BIBLE TIMES
Crafts for Kids

COMPILED BY
NEVA HICKERSON

Gospel Light

Billie Baptiste, Publisher
Dr. Elmer L. Towns, Senior Consulting Publisher
Gary S. Greig, Ph.D., Senior Editor, Bible and Theology
Neva Hickerson, Editor
Christy Weir, Consulting Editor
Phyllis Atchison, Assistant Editor
**Mary Gross, Brenda Kilgore, Pam Petropulos, Judy Roth, Dianne Rowell,
Laverne Kelvington Stroup, Kim Sullivan, Jan Worsham,** Contributing Writers
Eddi Fredrick, Sheryl Haystead, Contributing Editors
Carolyn Thomas, Designer
Chizuko Yasuda, Illustrator

Ideas for Chains and Hoop Earrings from *The Creative Factor*
by Laverne Kelvington Stroup, Christian Board of Publication,
St. Louis, Missouri. Used by permission.

© 1993 Gospel Light, Ventura, California 93006. All rights reserved. Printed in U.S.A.

Scripture quotations are from the Holy Bible, *New International Version.*
Copyright © 1973, 1978, 1984 International Bible Society.
Used by permission of Zondervan Bible Publishers.

Library of Congress Cataloging-in-Publication Data
Bible times crafts for kids / compiled by Neva Hickerson.
    p. cm.
  ISBN 0-8307-1596-7 : $12.99
  1. Bible crafts. 2. Handicrafts. I. Hickerson, Neva.
BS613.B485 1993
268'.432—dc20   92-31344
                                                      CIP

CONTENTS

SHALOM!
YOU'RE INVITED TO STEP BACK IN TIME—BACK TO BIBLE TIMES!

You and your students are invited to step back in time to experience the fascinating cultures of Bible Times. Prepare for the journey by making an entire Bible Times outfit including headpiece, tunic, belt, sandals and jewelry.

Openwork Headband

Tunic

Gold Armlet

Twisted-yarn Belt

Lace-up Sandals

Knotted Headband

Decorative Tassels

Cloth Belt

Beaded Anklet

Visit a Bible Times school and practice writing Hebrew words on ancient scrolls and tablets.

Participate in a Bible Times musical celebration using handmade lyres, flutes, tambourines and sistrums.

Tiny Clay Pot and Scroll

Clay Tablet

Hoop Earrings

Tambourine

Clay Bead Necklace

Lyre

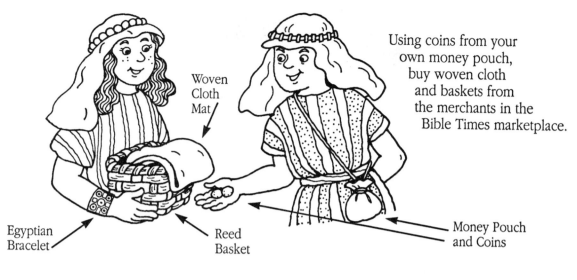

Using coins from your own money pouch, buy woven cloth and baskets from the merchants in the Bible Times marketplace.

Woven Cloth Mat

Egyptian Bracelet

Reed Basket

Money Pouch and Coins

Torch

Dramatize Bible stories, using props like a torch and chains.

Chain

And through the activities, learn about the people of Bible Times and their faith in God, who is the same "yesterday and today and forever." (Hebrews 13:8)

AGE LEVEL SYMBOLS

Next to the title of each project in this book you'll find the age level symbols shown below. These symbols tell what age children might enjoy doing each project. Symbols which are crossed out indicate a project is not appropriate for that age level. However, as you select projects, consider the particular children you are working with. Feel free to use your own ideas to make projects simpler or more difficult depending on the needs of your students.

YOUNG CHILDREN
Prekindergarten/Kindergarten

YOUNGER ELEMENTARY
Grades 1-3

OLDER ELEMENTARY
Grades 4-6

BIBLE TIMES CRAFTS CENTER

Have you tried the Activity Center approach to organizing your crafts program? Here's how it works:

▲ Designate one room in your church or school as the crafts center.

▲ Select craft projects that will appeal to several age levels. (Sometimes you'll find one project that all children will enjoy making. Other times you'll need to select one project for the younger children and one project for the older children.)

▲ Recruit adults or youth to assist you in preparing for and running the crafts center.

▲ Gather supplies.

▲ Decorate your room with Bible Times crafts such as clay pots, woven cloth, woven mats, simple musical instruments, Hebrew writing on scrolls, etc.

▲ Using ideas from this book, create Bible Times costumes for yourself and your assistants. Wear these costumes when you are working in the center.

▲ Designate a specific time of day when each class will visit the crafts center.

▲ As classes visit the crafts center, lead them in making projects, tailoring your instructions and conversation to the level of children you are working with.

CRAFTS WITH A MESSAGE

Every project in *Bible Times Crafts for Kids* includes a corresponding Bible verse. Many projects have drawings showing how that item was used in Bible Times. You may want to provide photocopies of verses and/or drawings for children to attach to their crafts. Below are some examples of ways to use verses and drawings to enhance the craft projects in this book.

GETTING READY

If you are planning to use crafts with a child at home, here are three helpful tips:

▲ Focus on the crafts in the book designated for your child's age, but don't ignore projects that are listed for older or younger ages. Elementary age children enjoy many of the projects geared for preschool and kindergarten children. And younger children are always interested in doing "big kid" things. Just plan on working along with the child, helping with tasks the child can't handle alone.

▲ Start with projects which call for materials you have around the house. Make a list of items you do not have which are needed for projects you think your child will enjoy. Plan to gather those supplies in one expedition.

▲ If certain materials seem too difficult to obtain, a little thought can usually lead to appropriate substitutions. And often the homemade version ends up being an improvement over the original plan.

If you are planning to lead a group of children in doing craft projects, keep these hints in mind:

▲ Choose projects which will allow children to work with a variety of materials.

▲ Make your selection of all projects far enough in advance to allow time to gather all needed supplies in one coordinated effort. Many projects use some of the same items.

▲ Make up a sample of each project to be sure the directions are fully understood and potential problems can be avoided. You may want to adapt some projects to simplify procedures or vary the materials required.

▲ Many items can be acquired as donations from people or businesses if you plan ahead and make your needs known. Many churches distribute lists of materials needed to their congregations and community and are able to provide crafts at little or no cost. Some items can be brought by the children themselves.

▲ In making your supplies list, distinguish between items which every individual child will need and those which will be shared among a group.

▲ Keep in mind that some materials may be shared among more than one age level, but only if there is good coordination among the groups. It is extremely frustrating to a teacher to expect to have scissors, only to discover another group is using them. Basic supplies which are used repeatedly in craft projects should usually be provided to every group.

ORDERING INFORMATION

To order bamboo and reeds, call or write to:
Frank's Cane and Rush Supply
7252 Heil Avenue
Huntington Beach, CA 92647
(714) 847-0707

To order additional craft supplies, contact:
Swanson, Inc., Dept. 200
1200 Park Avenue
Murfreesboro, TN 37133-1257
Questions: (615) 896-4114
Phone orders: 1-800-251-1402

HELPFUL HINTS

USING GLUE WITH YOUNG CHILDREN

Since preschoolers have difficulty using glue bottles effectively, you may want to try one of the following procedures. Purchase glue in large containers (up to one gallon size).

a. Pour a small amount of glue into several shallow containers.

b. Dilute glue by mixing a little water into each container.

c. Children use paste brushes to spread glue on project.

OR

a. Pour a small amount of glue into plastic margarine tub.

glue level →

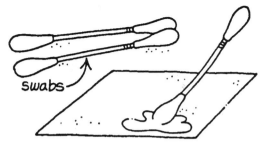

swabs

b. Give each child a cotton swab. The child dips the cotton swab into the glue and rubs glue on project.

c. Excess glue can be poured back into the large container at the end of each session.

CUTTING WITH SCISSORS

When cutting with scissors is required for these crafts, take note of the fact that some of the children in your class may be left-handed. It is very difficult for a left-handed person to cut with scissors that were designed to be used with the right hand. Have available in your classroom two or three pairs of left-handed scissors. These can be obtained from a school supply center.

BIBLE
TIMES
CLOTHING

TUNIC
(15 MINUTES)

Materials: Solid or striped cotton fabric in 45-inch (1.13-m) width, scissors, and measuring stick. (Children will need belts to hold the tunics in place. You may want to provide lengths of rope or cloth strips to use as belts. For other belt ideas, see pp. 11, 13).

Preparation: Measure and cut the fabric into 2-yard (1.8-m) lengths—one for each child. (You may want to adjust the length according to the height of children who will be wearing tunics.)

Instruct each child in the following procedures:

▲ Fold fabric rectangle in half (sketch a). Fold fabric in half again (sketch b).

▲ With teachers help, cut a quarter circle in the folded corner of the fabric to make a head hole (sketch c).

▲ Unfold fabric and try on tunic (sketch d). If the hole needs to be larger, refold fabric and cut a larger opening.

▲ Tie a cloth strip or length of rope around your waist to keep your tunic in place (sketch e).

Enrichment Ideas: Older children may enjoy using embroidery needles and yarn to sew a decorative stitch around neckline of tunic (see sketch). White or beige fabric may be dyed using natural dyes (see p. 12).

Life in Bible Times: What style of clothing is popular with kids your age? In Bible Times, men, women, boys and girls all wore the same type garment—a tunic. It was often made from a single piece of fabric woven on a wide loom. On a hot day, a loose tunic allowed air to circulate and help keep the body cool. On a cold day, the tunic could be wrapped around the body like a blanket to keep a person warm. At the end of the day, people didn't put on night clothes. They simply loosened their belts and slept with their tunics on.

"The man with two tunics should share with him who has none, and the one who has food should do the same." Luke 3:11

CLOTH BELT (GIRDLE)
(30 MINUTES)

Materials: Medium-weight, solid-colored fabric, scissors, measuring stick, yarn, embroidery needles, iron, ironing board.

Preparation: Cut fabric into 9x50-inch (22.5x125-cm) rectangles—one for each child. Fold the fabric into thirds (sketch a) and iron.

Instruct each child in the following procedures:

▲ Thread the needle with yarn. Push through all three thicknesses of fabric, about ¼ inch (.6 cm) from edge (sketch b).

▲ Cut yarn so 3 inches (7.5 cm) hangs on either side of fabric (sketch c).

▲ Tie yarn together with two small knots (sketch d).

▲ Repeat process to make fringe across both ends of the belt (sketch e).

▲ Tie belt around waist.

Simplification Idea: For younger children, teacher uses the hole punch to punch holes across ends of belts. Children thread precut yarn through each hole and knot (see sketch).

Enrichment Idea: Students sew two straight lines about 4 inches (10 cm) apart to form the pockets (see sketch).

Life in Bible Times: In Bible Times, people wore belts called girdles. The belts kept their tunics from opening and billowing while they walked or worked. Sometimes the girdle was slit to make a pocket for money or other small items. When men needed freedom of movement for working or running, they lifted the hems of their tunics and tucked them into their girdles. This was called "girding up the loins." This phrase came to mean being prepared. What do you think people in Bible Times needed to be prepared for?

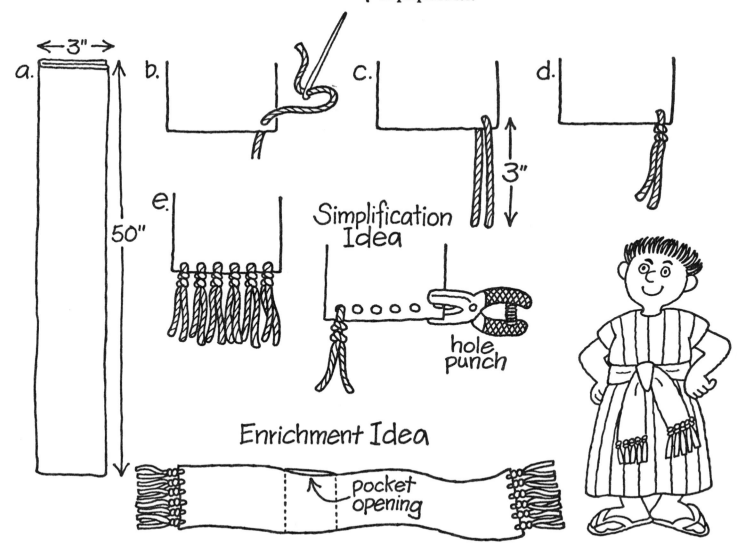

"Stand firm then, with the belt of truth buckled around your waist, with the breastplate of righteousness in place, and with your feet fitted with the readiness that comes from the gospel of peace." Ephesians 6:14,15

Natural Dyes
(30 MINUTES)

Materials: Large pot; water; wooden spoon; heating element; clothesline and clothespins; white, 100% cotton fabric; one or more of the following vegetables—red onion skins (to make pinkish-beige color); brown onion skins (yellowish beige); red cabbage (blue); red cabbage with vinegar (lavender); beets (deep pink). Note: Children may dye cloth used for making various projects in this book such as Head Covering, Tunic or Cloth Belt, or they may dye small swatches of cloth to experience effects of using various natural dyes.

Preparation: Fill pot half full of water. Bring pot of water to boil and add vegetables. Boil for 30 minutes to 1 hour. Remove vegetables.

Instruct each child in the following procedures:

▲ Carefully place the fabric in boiling water and stir with wooden spoon.

▲ When fabric has reached desired color (15-30 minutes), carefully lift from water.

▲ Do not rinse or wring out fabric.

▲ Hang fabric on a line and allow to dry.

▲ Optional—use dyed fabric to make Head Covering, Tunic or Cloth Belt projects.

Life in Bible Times: **What color clothes do you like to wear? In Bible Times, cloth was dyed various colors by boiling it in a pot of water with bark, nuts, vegetables, leaves or berries. The Bible tells about a woman named Lydia who sold purple cloth. Purple dye was made from the murex shellfish of the Mediterranean Sea. Only one drop of dye is found in each fish. Because it was rare and expensive, purple became the royal color worn by kings and noblemen and their families. King Solomon described the wife of a noble character who wore purple. The members of her household wore scarlet (red).**

"When it snows, she has no fear for her household; for all of them are clothed in scarlet....She is clothed in fine linen and purple." Proverbs 31:21,22

Twisted-Yarn Belt
(15 minutes)

Materials: Yarn in a variety of colors, scissors, measuring stick.

Preparation: Cut yarn into 3-yard (2.7-m) lengths—four for each child.

Instruct each child in the following procedures:

▲ Choose four lengths of yarn. Tie four lengths of yarn together with a knot at each end (sketch a).

▲ Choose a partner to work with. Partners stand facing one another, holding ends of yarn and pulling it taut (sketch b).

▲ Each child twists the yarn clockwise (to the right) until the yarn is tightly twisted and it begins to "kink."

▲ Give one child both ends of the yarn to hold. (Make sure yarn stays twisted.) The other child pulls on the center of the yarn and then lets go. The yarn should twist itself together, forming a rope (sketch c). If yarn does not twist, repeat previous step, twisting yarn even tighter.

▲ Tie one knot 2 inches (5 cm) from the previously tied knots, joining the yarn together (sketch d). Cut off original, smaller knots and untwist yarn to form tassel.

▲ Tie another knot 2 inches (5 cm) from the opposite end. Then cut through the yarn at the end of the loop to form a tassel on that end.

▲ Repeat process to make belt for the second child.

▲ Tie belt around waist.

Simplification Idea: Teacher ties knots for younger children.

Life in Bible Times: What kind of belts do you wear? In Bible Times, almost everyone wore a belt to keep his or her tunic in place. Some belts were made of woven cloth, others were made of leather. Kings sometimes wore belts made of gold!

"John's clothes were made of camel's hair, and he had a leather belt around his waist." Matthew 3:4

Decorative Tassels
(30 minutes)

Materials: Various colors of yarn, felt, scissors, glue, measuring stick. For each child—one 3x5-inch (7.5x12.5-cm) index card.

Preparation: Cut yarn into 6-foot (1.8-m) lengths—three for each child. Cut additional yarn into 5-inch (12.5-cm) lengths—three for each child. Cut additional yarn into 2-foot (60-cm) lengths—one for each child. Cut felt into 1x2-inch (2.5x5-cm) rectangles—three for each child.

Instruct each child in the following procedures:

▲ Wrap one 6-foot (1.8-m) length of yarn around index card (sketch a).

▲ Slip a 5-inch (12.5-cm) length of yarn between the yarn and the card and tie it tightly (sketch b).

▲ Cut through yarn at the untied edge (sketch b). Card will fall away.

▲ Glue felt rectangle around yarn near tied end (sketch c).

▲ Repeat to form two more tassels.

▲ Tie tassels near the center of 2-foot (.6-m) length of yarn.

▲ Knot yarn to form necklace.

Life in Bible Times: What kind of decorations are on your clothes? In Bible Times, people used tassels to decorate their clothes, baskets and tents. In the time of Moses, four tassels were sewn on each cloak. The tassels were to remind people of God's commands.

"The Lord said to Moses, 'Speak to the Israelites and say to them: "Throughout the generations to come you are to make tassels on the corners of your garments, with a blue cord on each tassel. You will have these tassels to look at and so you will remember all the commands of the Lord.'" Numbers 15:37-39

OPENWORK HEADBAND AND HEAD COVERING
(30 MINUTES)

Note: Young children will need extra help from the teacher to complete this project.

Materials: Solid or striped cotton fabric, sturdy cotton string or jute, plastic drinking straws in a variety of colors, measuring stick, transparent tape, scissors.

Preparation: Cut fabric into 1-yard (90-cm) squares—one for each child. Cut string into 1-yard (90-cm) lengths—two for each child. Tie two lengths of string together about 8 inches (20 cm) from one end (sketch a). Wrap each untied end of string with tape to make "needles" (sketch a). Cut drinking straws into 1-inch (2.5-cm) lengths—10-14 for each child.

Instruct each child in the following procedures:

▲ Thread one length of string through a straw piece (sketch b).
▲ Entering from the opposite end, thread second length of string through same straw piece (sketch c).
▲ Pull both lengths of string to move straw close to knot.
▲ Repeat process to add remaining straw pieces.
▲ Tie a knot to hold straw pieces in place (sketch d).
▲ Knot all four loose ends of the string to keep them from unraveling.
▲ Fold fabric to make a triangle. Place fold across forehead with two points on either side of head and one point center back. With teacher's help, tie headband around your head to keep your head covering in place (sketch e).

Life in Bible Times: **What type of hat do you wear when you're out in the sun? In Bible Times, most people wore some kind of cloth to protect their heads from the heat of the sun. To keep the cloth in place, people wore headbands. Some headbands were similar to the one you're making.**

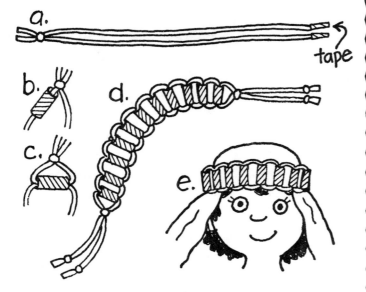

"Bring his sons and dress them in tunics and put headbands on them. Then tie sashes on Aaron and his sons." Exodus 29:8,9

MARRIED WOMAN'S HEADBAND
(30 MINUTES)

Materials: Solid or striped cotton fabric, heavy thread, measuring stick, scissors, iron, ironing board. For each child—one sewing needle, 5-10 metal washers (flat cut and fender types).

Preparation: Cut fabric into 5x45-inch (12.5x112.5-cm) rectangles—one for each child. Fold edges of each fabric rectangle towards center and press (sketch a). Fold in half lengthwise so pressed edges are aligned and raw edges are inside (sketch b). Press.

Instruct each child in the following procedures:

▲ Cut a long length of thread. Thread needle and knot thread.
▲ Beginning at center of headband, sew "coins" (washers) to headband (sketch c).
▲ With teacher's help, tie headband around your head.

Life in Bible Times: **What do most women today wear to show they are married? (Wedding ring.) In Bible Times, a woman often wore her wedding gift coins on her clothes or headband to show that she was married. The coins also showed how rich she was. To her, these coins were something like the diamonds in a woman's wedding band. Jesus told a parable (story) about a woman searching for a lost coin. For her, losing a coin was something like losing a diamond from her wedding ring.**

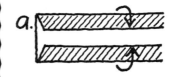

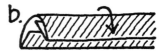

"Or suppose a woman has ten silver coins and loses one. Does she not light a lamp, sweep the house and search carefully until she finds it?" Luke 15:8

KNOTTED HEADBAND AND HEAD COVERING
(60 MINUTES)

Materials: Solid or striped cotton fabric, jute or twine, measuring stick, scissors, pony beads—six for each child.

Preparation: Cut fabric into 1-yard (90-cm) squares—one for each child. Cut jute into 1-yard (90-cm) lengths—two for each child. Cut additional jute into 3-yard (2.7-m) lengths—two for each child.

Instruct each child in the following procedures:

▲ Line up four lengths of jute (two long, two short) and tie an overhand knot about 6 inches (15 cm) from end (sketch a).

▲ With the two longer strands on outside and the two shorter strands on inside, tie a square knot (sketches b and c).

▲ Tie five more square knots, keeping shorter strands on the inside. Then slide one bead onto the center two strands of jute. Slide bead up to knot (sketch d).

▲ Repeat the previous two steps until all six beads have been used. After putting on the sixth bead, tie six square knots and one overhand knot to complete headband.

▲ Fold fabric to make a triangle. Place fold across forehead with two points on either side of head and one point center back. Tie headband around forehead to hold fabric in place.

Life in Bible Times: **What type of hats do you like to wear? In Bible Times, head coverings were worn by both men and women to protect their heads from the wind, sun and rain. A woman's headpiece often had a small pad placed on top to help her balance jars she carried on her head.**

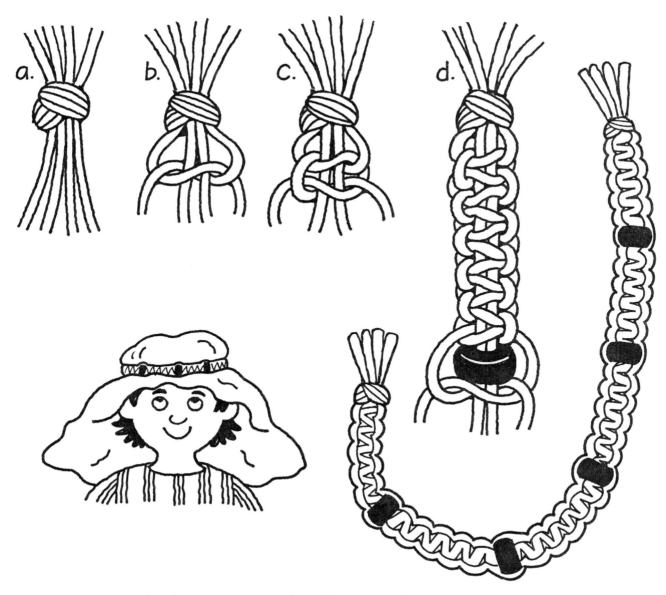

"But you are a shield around me, O Lord; you bestow glory on me and lift up my head." Psalm 3:3

LACE-UP SANDALS
(30 MINUTES)

Materials: Corrugated cardboard, pencils, brown felt, scissors, measuring stick, craft knife, black felt pens, glue, 3/4-inch (1.9-cm) brown ribbon or bias tape.

Preparation: Cut cardboard into 10-inch (25-cm) squares—two for each child. Cut felt into 10-inch (25-cm) squares—two for each child. Cut ribbon into 1½-yard (1.35-m) lengths—two for each child.

Instruct each child in the following procedures:

▲ Trace around your shoes onto cardboard squares and cut out (sketch a).

▲ Trace around cardboard shoe shapes onto felt and cut out.

▲ Glue felt to cardboard shoe shapes to make sandal soles (sketch b).

▲ With your shoes off, stand on sandal soles. Teacher marks 6 spots for slits on each sole (sketch c). Slits should be 3/4-inch (1.9-cm) long and at least 1/4-inch (.6-cm) from edge of sole. Teacher then uses craft knife to cut slits.

▲ Beginning at toes, thread ribbon from under sole through slits (sketch d). Complete lacing as shown (sketches e and f). Repeat to lace second sandal.

Life in Bible Times: What kind of shoes are popular with kids your age? In Bible Times, most people wore sandals made of leather. On dry days, people's feet were dusty and on wet days they were muddy. For this reason, it was common for people to remove their shoes when going inside a house. Then a servant would wash their feet. Jesus did the work of a servant when He washed the disciples' feet.

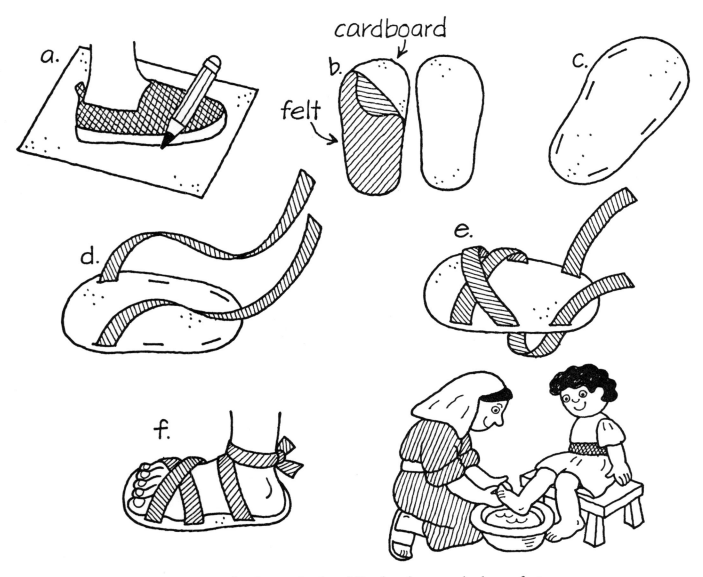

"Now that I, your Lord and Teacher, have washed your feet,
you also should wash one another's feet." John 13:14

SLIP-ON SANDALS
(30 MINUTES)

Materials: Sandal Sole Patterns, lightweight cardboard or brown poster board, leather or plastic lacing (lanyard), ¾-inch (1.9-cm) elastic, heavy duty thread, large needle, felt pen, hole punches, scissors, craft knife, measuring stick.

Preparation: At least one day before children will make sandals, have children stand on Sandal Sole Patterns to determine which size soles each child will need. Using pattern as a guide, cut soles from cardboard—four for each child. Using pattern as a guide, mark dots where holes are to be punched around each sole. (Holes must be in the same place on each sole.) Use craft knife to make slits in two of the soles in each set of four (sketch a). Cut lacing into 30-inch (75-cm) lengths—two for each child. Cut elastic into 7-inch (17.5-cm) lengths—four for each child. Note: For large soles, cut 40-inch (100-cm) laces and 8-inch (20-cm) elastic. Thread elastic through slits in soles, overlap on underside of sole and stitch together (sketch b).

Instruct each child in the following procedures:

▲ Use hole punch to make holes around the sandal where indicated.

▲ Lay sole with elastic straps on top of sole without straps. With teacher's help, thread lacing through two holes and tie a knot (sketch c).

▲ Always entering holes through the top of sandal, lace all the way around sole (sketch d).

▲ When finished lacing, tie a knot to secure.

▲ Repeat to lace second sandal.

Enrichment Idea: Older children use needle and thread to stitch elastic together.

Life in Bible Times: **What kind of shoes do you like to wear? In Bible Times, most people wore sandals made of leather. The sandals were made by a tanner. The tanner sat at a low bench to work. He used a knife to cut the leather. Then he used a needle and waxed linen thread to sew leather pieces together.**

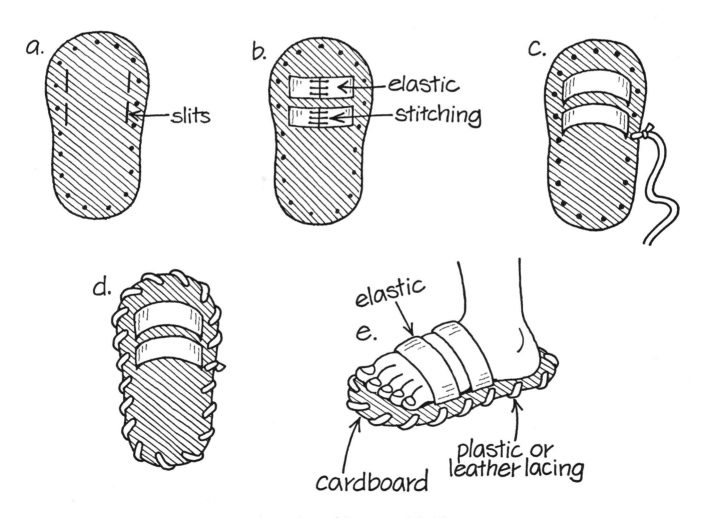

"How beautiful your sandaled feet,
O prince's daughter!" Song of Songs 7:1

SANDAL SOLE PATTERNS

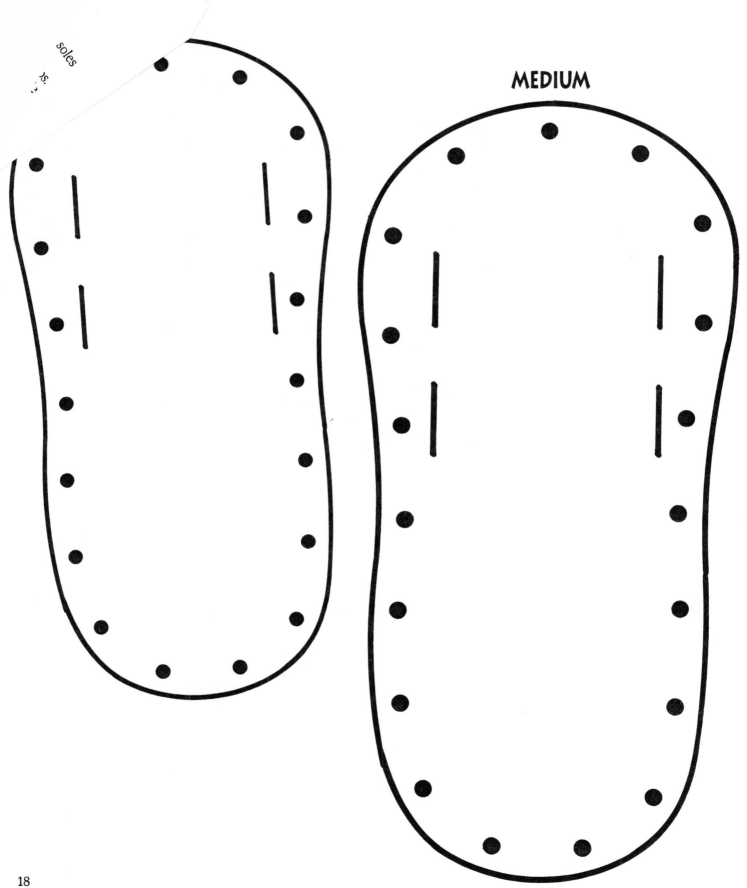

soles

MEDIUM

SANDAL SOLE PATTERN

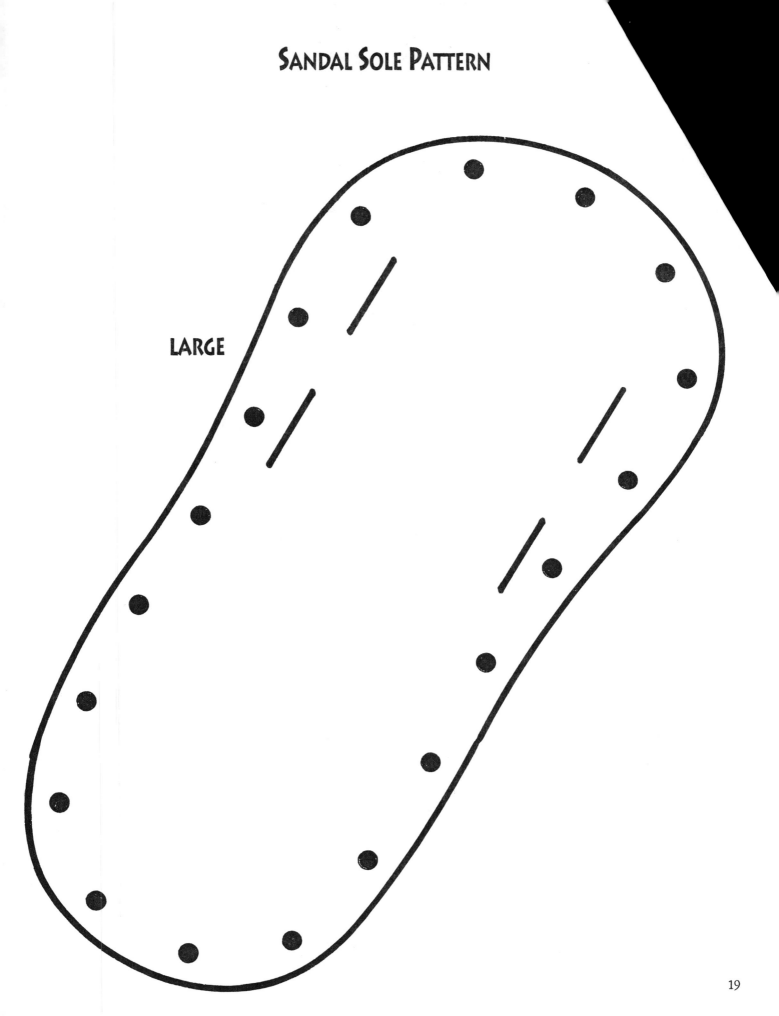

LARGE

PRIEST'S BREASTPLATE
(30 MINUTES)

...d red felt; measuring stick; ...ple seam binding; needles; pur-...-twelve ½-inch (1.25-cm) acrylic ...ie side) in gold, purple, blue, red. ...purple felt into 6x8½-inch (15x21.25-cm) ...for each child. Cut blue, gold and red felt into ...(2.5x3.75-cm) rectangles—12 for each child (four ...n color). Cut seam binding into 2-foot (.6-m) lengths—...ur for each child.

Instruct each child in the following procedures:

▲ Arrange 12 felt pieces on purple rectangle (see sketch) and glue to secure.
▲ Glue an acrylic jewel in the center of each small felt piece.
▲ Thread needle. Fold under end of one length of seam bind-

ing and stitch to corner of purple felt rectangle.
▲ Stitch a length of seam binding to remaining corners of the rectangle.
▲ With teacher's help, tie breastplate around neck and waist.

Life in Bible Times: **In Bible Times, priests were the spiritual leaders of God's people. They taught the people how to worship God. The high priest wore a special tunic or robe made of multi-colored material. Over the tunic, he wore a gold, blue, purple and scarlet breastplate made of linen. The breastplate had 12 stones attached to it. Each stone was a symbol of one of the 12 tribes of Israel. The stones were a reminder to the priest of his responsibility before God as a spiritual leader of the tribes. The very first high priest was Aaron, the brother of Moses.**

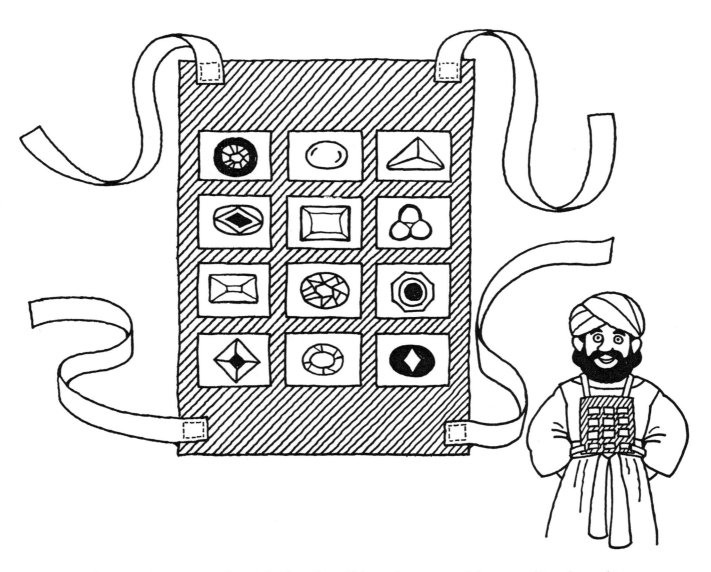

"Whenever Aaron enters the Holy Place, he will bear the names of the sons of Israel over his heart on the breastpiece of decision as a continuing memorial before the Lord." Exodus 28:29

BIBLE TIMES JEWELRY

SIGNET RING
(60 MINUTES)

...ng compound (Sculpy or ...ply stores) in metallic or neu- ..., ½-inch (1.25-cm) dowels, saw, ... foil, plastic knives, sealing wax ...ores), matches, notepaper, pens. Op- ...t in metallic colors (gold, silver, platinum, ...brushes.

...ation: Divide modeling compound into ½-ounce por- ...ons—one for each child. Cut dowels into 2-inch (5-cm) lengths—one for each child. Line baking sheets with foil. Cut a sheet of wax paper for each child to work on. Preheat oven according to directions on modeling compound package.

Instruct each child in the following procedures:

▲ Knead clay (modeling compound) until it is soft and pliable.

▲ Use a portion of the clay to form a ball about the size of a marble (sketch a).

▲ Flatten ball onto wax paper until it is about the size of a nickle (sketch b).

▲ Use remaining clay to make a rope about 2 inches (5 cm) long.

▲ Wrap rope around dowel, pushing ends together to secure (sketch c).

▲ Remove flattened ball of clay from wax paper and press it onto the ring on the dowel (sketch d).

▲ Make a thin clay rope. Use this rope to form your initial. (If necessary, use a plastic knife to cut small pieces.)

▲ Lay initial BACKWARDS onto flattened part of ring (sketch e). The initial must be backwards on ring in order to come out correctly when impression is made in wax. Lightly press initial into ring.

▲ Place ring (still on dowel) on baking sheet. Bake in pre-heated oven for 15-25 minutes.

▲ Allow to cool completely, then remove dowel.

▲ While ring is baking and cooling, use notepaper and pen to write a note to someone. If time allows, write several notes.

▲ Fold paper into three sections (sketch f).

▲ Optional: Paint ring with metallic-colored paint. Allow to dry.

▲ Melt sealing wax (about the size of a quarter) onto paper.

▲ Press ring into wax to make an impression (sketch g).

Enrichment Idea: A decorative twisted rope may be added to the ring, encircling the signet. Make two very thin ropes and twist them together. Press the twisted rope firmly around the edge of the clay circle.

Life in Bible Times: Signet rings were worn by kings and wealthy citizens in Bible Times and were highly valued objects. Some rings had writing embossed on them. Others were embossed with tiny portraits of their owners. Kings pressed their rings into wax seals on important documents. This showed that the document was approved by the king. No one else had a seal exactly like the king's. If a king loaned or gave his signet ring to someone, he was giving that person authority to make important decisions.

a. b. c. d. e. f. g. sealing wax paper or envelope

Enrichment Idea

"So Pharaoh said to Joseph, 'I hereby put you in charge of the whole land of Egypt.' Then Pharaoh took his signet ring from his finger and put it on Joseph's finger. He dressed him in robes of fine linen and put a gold chain around his neck." Genesis 41:41,42

JEWELED PENDANT NECKLACE
(60 MINUTES)

Materials: Oven-hardening modeling compound (Sculpy or Fimo brand, available at craft supply stores) in metallic or neutral colors, oven, baking sheets, thin gold or silver cording, toothpicks, measuring stick, assorted acrylic rhinestones in various shapes and colors, glue, scissors, acrylic paint in metallic colors (gold, silver, platinum, bronze), paintbrushes, small cups for paint. For each child—one small metal cookie tart pan or candy mold.

Preparation: Cut cord into 2-foot (60-cm) lengths—one for each child. Divide 2-ounce packages of clay (modeling compound) into two or three portions, depending on the size of the molds to be used. Pour paint into small cups. Preheat oven according to instructions on modeling compound package.

Instruct each child in the following procedures:

▲ Knead clay until it is soft and pliable.

▲ Press clay into metal mold, covering the bottom and sides (sketch a). Press in firmly.

▲ Use toothpick to make a hole near the top of the molded clay (sketch b). The hole should be large enough for two strands of cord to pass through.

▲ Place mold on baking sheet and bake for 15-25 minutes.

▲ Allow to cool. Then remove clay from mold.

▲ Paint pendant with metallic-colored paint. Allow to dry.

▲ Thread the gold or silver cording through the hole in the top of the pendant (sketch c). Tie cord at ends to secure.

▲ Glue rhinestones onto pendant.

Life in Bible Times: In Bible Times, goldsmiths and silversmiths made beautiful jewelry. First they placed the raw metal in a small pottery bowl and heated it over hot charcoal. Then they poured the liquid gold or silver into a mold made of stone. After the metal cooled, it was removed from the mold and made into a piece of jewelry. The mold could be used again and again.

"Then the servant brought out gold and silver jewelry and articles of clothing and gave them to Rebekah." Genesis 24:53

Egyptian Bracelets
(30 MINUTES)

Materials: Scissors, aluminum foil, oven or electric griddle, baking sheets, acrylic rhinestones, toilet paper tubes or paper towel tubes, ruler. For each child—one 1½x7-inch (3.75x17.5-cm) length of Friendly Plastic in gold, copper, silver or bronze. (Friendly Plastic is a craft plastic used for making jewelry and is available at craft supply stores.)

Preparation: Use scissors to cut Friendly Plastic into 5-inch (12.5-cm) lengths—one for each child. Save scraps. Cut foil into 4x6-inch (10x15-cm) rectangles—one for each child. If using the oven—preheat oven to 400 degrees. If using the griddle—preheat to medium heat.

Instruct each child in the following procedures:

▲ Place plastic rectangle in center of foil piece.

▲ From scraps of plastic in contrasting colors, cut shapes (circles, squares, triangles) to decorate your bracelet. Optional: Cut out representations of things in nature such as fish, trees, mountains, flowers, etc.

▲ Arrange shapes on top of plastic rectangle (sketch a).

▲ Carefully pick up the foil and plastic and place on the griddle or baking sheet.

▲ If using oven, bake for about 30-60 seconds, watching carefully. Bake only long enough for shapes to melt and bond to the rectangle.

▲ If using griddle, allow to remain on griddle about 60 seconds or until shapes look softened and are slightly melted.

▲ Remove from heat source and place rhinestones on the bracelet wherever desired (sketch b). Push into the softened plastic.

▲ While plastic is still warm, wrap foil and plastic around a cardboard tube, aligning ends of plastic (sketch c).

▲ Allow to cool completely. Slip bracelet off tube, then peel away the foil.

Life in Bible Times: In Egypt, both men and women wore bracelets made from gold and silver. Women sometimes wore several bracelets on each arm. The designs on Egyptian jewelry often told stories. Sometimes designs were simple drawings, geometric shapes or patterns representing things in nature.

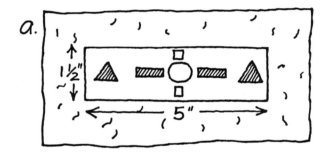

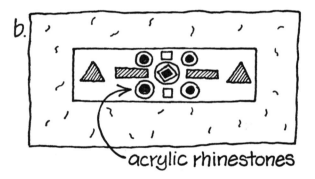

acrylic rhinestones

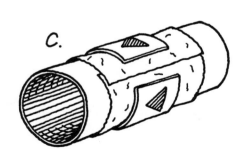

"A word aptly spoken is like apples of gold in settings of silver." Proverbs 25:11

BEADED EARRINGS
(60 MINUTES)

Materials: Colored glass seed beads, gold-tone ball beads, gold-tone specialty beads (mushroom, faceted, antiqued, etc.), needle nose pliers, small cups. For each child—six 2-inch (5-cm) brass or gold-tone headpins, two brass jump rings, two gold fishhook earring findings or gold clip earring findings with loops attached for hanging beads, one dishcloth or fabric scrap on which to work. Note: Beads and other supplies for making earrings are available at craft supply stores.

Preparation: Place each type of bead in a separate cup.

Instruct each child in the following procedures:

▲ Choose the beads you want to use. Use at least three different types of beads.

▲ Place beads on the first headpin, using a repeating pattern. Example: 1 gold bead, 4 blue beads, 1 mushroom bead, 4 blue beads, repeat (sketch a). Leave top ½ inch (1.25 cm) of headpin free of beads.

▲ Using needle nose pliers, grasp tip of the head pin and curve the wire into an *O* shape. Close circle (sketch b).

▲ Using same bead pattern or a variation, repeat process on remaining five headpins.

▲ Use pliers to open one jump ring. Thread the three beaded headpins onto the jump ring (sketch c).

▲ Use pliers to close jump ring, making ends meet.

▲ Open loop on earring finding and slip on jump ring (sketch d). Close the loop securely (sketch e).

▲ Repeat to make second earring.

Life in Bible Times: Ancient Egyptians heated a mixture of quartz, sand, potash or soda and lime and used this material to make beads. Even today beads are made from the same materials. Ancient Egyptian women had pierced ears and wore fishhook earrings much like the ones people wear today. Ancient Egyptian fishhook earrings can be seen today in archaeological museums.

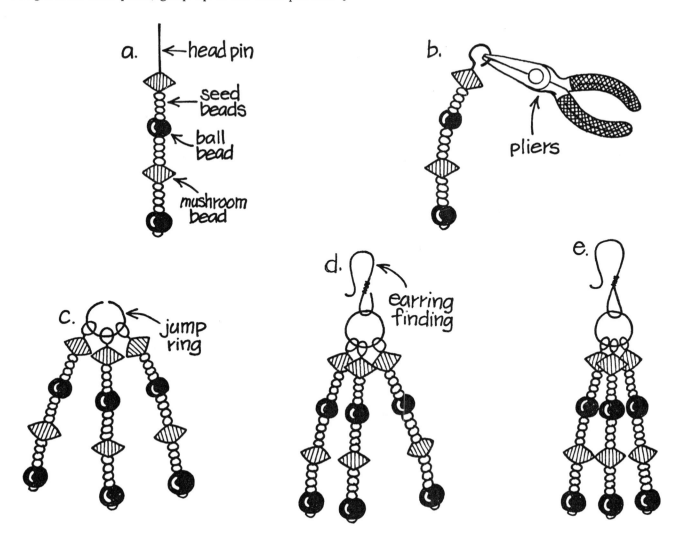

"Like an earring of gold or an ornament of fine gold is a wise man's rebuke to a listening ear." Proverbs 25:12

GOLD ARMLETS AND BRACELETS
(30 MINUTES)

Materials: Toilet paper tubes or paper towel tubes, metallic gold acrylic spray paint, a variety of gold fabric trim (rickrack, braid, cord, etc.), acrylic rhinestones, ruler, pencil, craft glue, scissors, newspapers, paper clips.

Preparation: Cut tubes into 2-inch (5-cm) hoops—two for each child. Use scissors to cut an opening in each hoop (sketch a). Lay hoops on newspaper in outside area and spray paint gold. Cut gold trim into 5½-inch (13.75-cm) lengths (or circumference of tube). Cover work area with newspaper.

Instruct each child in the following procedures:

▲ Squeeze a line of glue along edge of one armlet or bracelet.

▲ Press a length of gold trim onto line of glue (sketch b). While drying, secure trim with paper clips.

▲ Repeat previous step to add gold trim to the other edge of tube.

▲ Add additional rows of trim as desired.

▲ Glue several acrylic rhinestones to bracelet (sketch c).

▲ Allow to dry.

▲ Decorate second bracelet.

Life in Bible Times: What types of jewelry do women wear today? What types of jewelry do men wear? In Bible Times, both men and women wore bracelets and armlets made from gold and silver. Bracelets were worn on the wrist and armlets were worn on the top part of the arm above the elbow.

a. cut

b.

c.

"So we have brought as an offering to the Lord the gold articles each of us acquired—armlets, bracelets, signet rings, earrings and necklaces." Numbers 31:50

HOOP EARRINGS
(15 MINUTES)

Materials: Toilet paper tubes or paper towel tubes, scissors, ruler, gold spray paint, yarn, small acrylic jewels (which are flat on one side), glue, glitter, newspaper.

Preparation: Cut tubes into ½-inch (1.25-cm) hoops—two for each child. Lay hoops on newspaper in an outside area and spray paint gold. Cut the yarn into 12-inch (30-cm) lengths—two for each child. Cover the work area with newspaper.

Instruct each child in the following procedures:

▲ Glue several jewels on each gold hoop.

▲ Decorate hoops with dots or lines of glitter.

▲ Thread a length of yarn through each hoop and tie.

▲ To wear earrings, hang yarn loops over ears.

Life in Bible Times: What type of jewelry do you like to wear? In Bible Times, women and girls wore earrings made of gold and silver. By looking at a woman's earrings, people could tell if she was rich or poor.

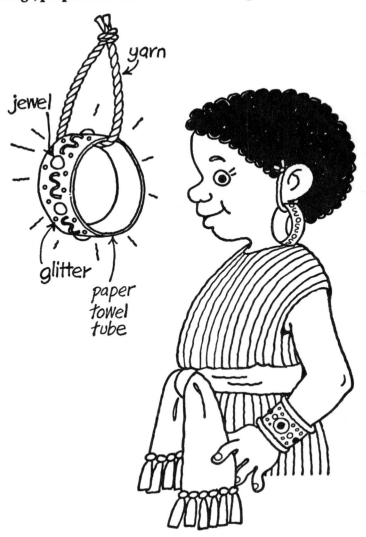

yarn

jewel

glitter

paper towel tube

"We will make you earrings of gold, studded with silver." Song of Songs 1:11

26

BEADED BRACELET AND ANKLET
(15 MINUTES)

Materials: Metallic pony beads, acrylic faceted beads in jewel-tone colors (available at craft supply stores), scissors. For each child—two 12-inch (30-cm) gold or silver chenille wires.

Instruct each child in the following procedures:

▲ String beads (about 10) onto chenille wire (sketch a).

▲ Bend the wire into a circle and try on wrist. If bracelet is too large, trim off a section of wire.

▲ Twist ends of chenille wire together.

▲ Repeat process to make anklet.

Life in Bible Times: In Bible Times, children wore bangles on their wrists and ankles. They were often made out of long pieces of metal called bronze. The bronze was beaten and then bent to the right size for a child's wrist or ankle. Isaac's servant gave Rebekah nose rings and bracelets.

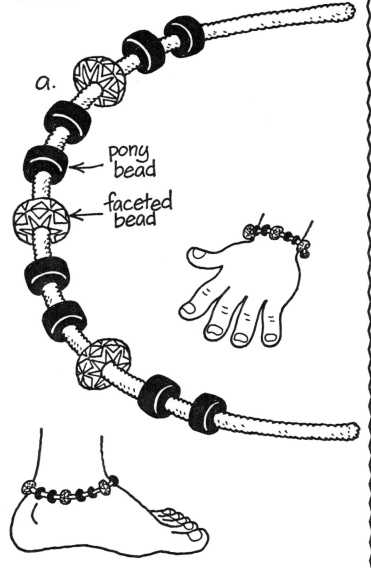

a.

pony bead

faceted bead

"Then I put the ring in her nose and the bracelets on her arms." Genesis 24:47

REED BRACELET
(15 MINUTES)

Note: Young children will need extra teacher help to complete this project.

Materials: Number 2 round reed (see p. 7 for ordering instructions), clothespins, bucket of water, towel.

Preparation: Separate reed coil into single strands. Recoil single strands and clip each coil with a clothespin. Soak in a bucket of water for 3-5 minutes. Remove clothespins.

Instruct each child in the following procedures:

▲ Using the end of one reed, make a circle about 1 inch (2.5 cm) larger than your wrist (sketch a).

▲ Using opposite end of reed, weave strand in and out of the circle three or four times (sketch b).

▲ Continue winding reed in and out of circle until entire length of reed has been used (sketch c).

▲ Make additional bracelets as time allows.

Life in Bible Times: What plants grow near your house or apartment? In Bible Times, plants called reeds grew along the Nile River in Egypt. They were used to make baskets and mats. Reeds were also used to make pens. When Moses was a baby his mother hid him in a basket among the reeds on the Nile.

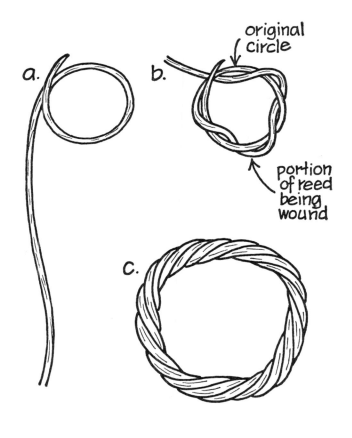

a.

b. original circle

portion of reed being wound

c.

"Then she placed the child in [the basket] and put it among the reeds along the bank of the Nile." Exodus 2:3

CLAY BEAD NECKLACE WITH MEDALLION
(TWO-DAY PROJECT/30 MINUTES)

Materials: Air-drying clay, Cornstarch Dough or Sawdust Clay (see recipes on p. 51), plastic drinking straws, scissors, measuring stick, sharp pencils or nails, one or more of the following—yarn, metallic cord or leather lacing. Optional—tempera paint and paintbrushes.

Preparation: Divide clay into fist-sized portions—one for each child. Cut yarn, cord or lacing into 2-foot (60-cm) lengths—one for each child.

Instruct each child in the following procedures:

DAY ONE:

▲ Make several small balls of clay for beads.

▲ Push a straw through the middle of each bead (sketch a). Beads will dry in place on the straw.

▲ Make a larger ball of clay and flatten to ½-inch (1.25-cm) for medallion.

▲ Use straw to make hole through top of medallion (sketch b).

▲ Use pencil or nail to draw letters or symbols in the medallion.

▲ Allow beads and medallion to dry in sun for several days.

DAY TWO:

▲ Optional—paint beads and medallion and allow to dry.

▲ Thread beads and medallion on a length of yarn, cording or leather lacing.

▲ Tie necklace around your neck.

Life in Bible Times: Do you wear necklaces or bracelets? In Bible Times, clothing was simple and jewelry was one of the only ways to dress up and wear something special. Where do you get your jewelry? In Bible Times, some people made their own jewelry. Others went to the marketplace and bought jewelry or traded other goods for jewelry.

a. clay ball   drinking straw

side view

b.

c.

"Then at Belshazzar's command, Daniel was clothed in purple, a gold chain was placed around his neck, and he was proclaimed the third highest ruler in the kingdom." Daniel 5:29

BIBLE TIMES MUSICAL INSTRUMENTS

TAMBOURINE
(30 MINUTES)

Materials: Hammers, large nails, masking tape, ruler, scissors, craft knife, oatmeal boxes, wood-grain adhesive paper, scrap wood. For each child—six frozen juice can lids and three standard-size paper clips.

Preparation: Use craft knife to cut 2¼-inch (5.6-cm) cylinders from the oatmeal boxes—one for each child (sketch a). Cut three 3x¾-inch (7.5x1.9-cm) rectangular holes spaced evenly around each cylinder (sketch a). Cut adhesive paper into 1½x16-inch (3.75x40-cm) strips—two for each child. Cut additional adhesive paper into ¾x6-inch (1.9x15-cm) strips—three for each child.

Instruct each child in the following procedures:

▲ Lay juice can lids on scrap-wood surface. Use hammer and nail to make a hole in center of each lid (sketch b).
▲ Straighten one end of each paper clip so only one bend remains. Thread two juice can lids onto each paper clip (sketch c). The sharp edges of nail holes should face each other.
▲ Center lids in rectangular cut-outs and hook paper clips to edges of cylinder. Use masking tape to secure (sketch d).
▲ Peel backing off shorter adhesive paper strips and wrap around sections between cut-outs on cylinder (sketch e).
▲ Use longer adhesive strips to cover the rims of cylinder (sketch f).
▲ Shake tambourine and hit against palm to play.

Life in Bible Times: **In Bible Times, tambourines were usually played by women. They kept the rhythm going as people danced to celebrate or worship. Miriam sang and danced with a tambourine to celebrate after the Hebrews made it through the Red Sea. What do you like to do when you're very happy?**

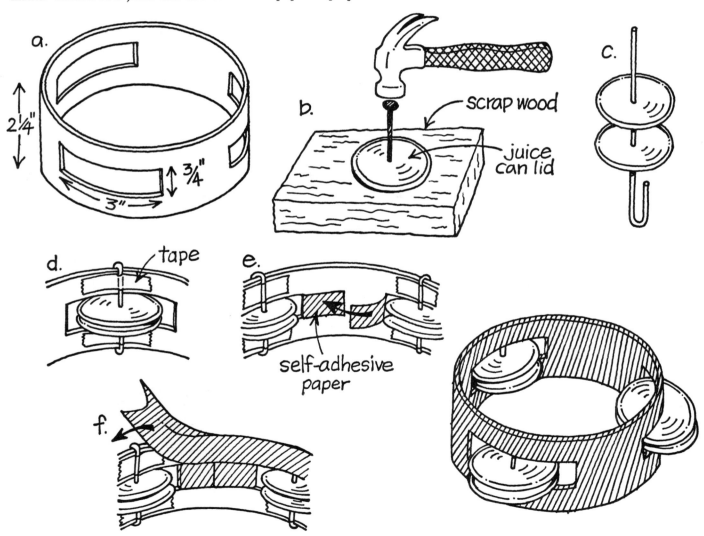

"Then Miriam the prophetess, Aaron's sister, took a tambourine in her hand, and all the women followed her, with tambourines and dancing." Exodus 15:20

CYMBALS
(15 MINUTES)

Materials: Felt, ruler, scissors, permanent felt pens in a variety of colors. For each child—two 9-inch (22.5-cm) aluminum pie pans and four paper fasteners (brads).

Preparation: Cut felt into 2x5-inch (5x12.5-cm) strips—two for each child.

Instruct each child in the following procedures:

▲ Use felt pens to decorate your cymbals (sketch a).

▲ With teacher's help, use paper fasteners to attach felt handles to backs of cymbals (sketch b).

▲ Hold cymbals by handles and hit them together to play (sketch c).

Life in Bible Times: Cymbals are rhythm instruments made of metal. Hitting the metal pieces together makes a very loud sound. In Bible Times, cymbals were played when people worshiped God at the Temple. Cymbals were played at the beginning or ending of a song or during the pauses of the song (when people weren't singing). Why do you think cymbals weren't played while people were singing?

"David and the whole house of Israel were celebrating with all their might before the Lord, with songs and with harps, lyres, tambourines, sistrums and cymbals." 2 Samuel 6:5

TRUMPET
(15 MINUTES)

Materials: Discarded garden hose, heavy-duty shears, scissors, masking tape, ruler, aluminum foil, permanent felt pens in a variety of colors. For each child—one plastic funnel.

Preparation: Cut hose into 10-inch (25-cm) lengths—one for each child. Cut foil into 20-inch (50-cm) lengths—one for each child.

Instruct each child in the following procedures:

▲ Place hose length over small end of funnel (sketch a).

▲ Wrap masking tape around end of hose and end of funnel to secure them together (sketch b).

▲ Use felt pens to color shiny side of foil.

▲ Wrap funnel and hose with aluminum foil, shiny side out.

▲ To play, blow into pipe and make a "trumpet sound."

Life in Bible Times: In Bible Times, trumpets were made of silver or bronze. They were played to make announcements on special days. A trumpet might be played to tell people it was time to come to a big party or to tell soldiers it was time to start a battle. The Bible tells us that when Jesus returns to take us to heaven, we will hear a loud trumpet sound. What would you like to announce with your trumpet?

"They will see the Son of Man coming on the clouds of the sky, with power and great glory. And he will send his angels with a loud trumpet call." Matthew 24:30,31

SISTRUM
(15 MINUTES)

Materials: Wire cutter, pliers, fine-gauge wire, measuring stick, crepe paper streamers in bright colors, scissors, glue, transparent tape. For each child—one wire coat hanger and eight colorful buttons.

Preparation: Bend the hooked end of each hanger into a long closed loop (sketch a). Cut off bottom section of wire on hanger (sketch b). Bend remaining wires to form a wishbone shape (sketch c). Use pliers to twist the ends of wire into small closed loops (sketch d). Cut fine-gauge wire into 1-foot (30-cm) lengths—one for each child. Cut crepe paper into 2-foot (60-cm) lengths—one for each child.

Instruct each child in the following procedures:

▲ Twist one end of wire length around one of the small loops on hanger (sketch e).

▲ Thread buttons onto wire.

▲ Twist loose end of wire around second loop on hanger, making it as tight as possible.

▲ Wind crepe paper up and down around the base of hanger to cover handle. Before winding paper around for the last time, squeeze a line of glue down the middle to secure paper in place (sketch f). Press end of paper in place. Tape end of paper to secure.

▲ To play, shake sistrum to make a rattling sound.

Life in Bible Times: **Can you name some percussion instruments?** (Drums, tambourine, cymbals, triangle, timpani, blocks, bongos.) **The sistrum was an Egyptian percussion instrument used in Bible Times. It was made of metal and usually had an oval loop with cross-pieces. The cross-pieces held loose rings that jangled together when the sistrum was shaken.**

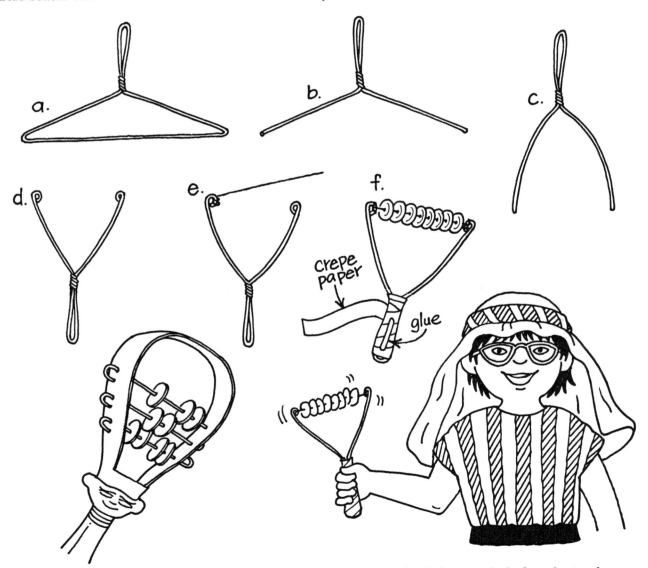

"David and the whole house of Israel were celebrating with all their might before the Lord, with songs and with harps, lyres, tambourines, sistrums and cymbals." 2 Samuel 6:5

LYRE
(30 MINUTES)

Materials: Wood-grain adhesive paper, measuring stick, scissors, transparent tape. For each child—one tissue box (most any size will work), two pencil-sized twigs, five large rubber bands of varying widths.

Preparation: Measure and cut adhesive paper to cover tissue box—one for each child.

Instruct each child in the following procedures:

▲ Remove backing and wrap self-adhesive paper around tissue box. Make sure seam is on bottom of box.

▲ Fold ends as if you were wrapping a package and tape to secure (sketch a).

▲ Cut slashes in adhesive paper where it covers opening in box (sketch b). Fold back cut paper to reveal opening (sketch c).

▲ Stretch rubber bands lengthwise around box.

▲ Carefully insert a twig underneath rubber bands on each end of box (sketch d).

▲ Pluck and strum bands to play lyre.

Life in Bible Times: What instrument do you know how to play? What instrument would you like to learn? Many people in Bible Times played small harps called lyres. Lyres were stringed instruments with wooden frames. The strings were made from the intestines of birds. One boy who played a lyre was a shepherd named David. He probably took his lyre along when caring for his sheep and played it at night to pass the time. King Saul hired David to play the lyre for him. The music soothed the king when he was in a bad mood. When you're in a bad mood, what helps you feel better?

"I will sing a new song to you, O God; on the ten-stringed lyre I will make music to you." Psalm 144:9

SHEPHERD'S FLUTE
(30 MINUTES)

Materials: Bamboo (see p. 7 for ordering information), utility knife, felt pen, rulers, hammers, nails, saw, sandpaper.

Preparation: Beginning about ½-inch (1.25-cm) below plugged joint, saw bamboo into 10- to 12-inch (25- to 30-cm) lengths—one for each child. One end of each length should be plugged and one end should be open. Use utility knife to whittle a v-shaped notch in open end of each bamboo length (sketch a).

Instruct each child in the following procedures:

▲ Use sandpaper to sand rough edges of flute.

▲ On the notched side of pipe, beginning 1 inch (2.5 cm) from plugged end, use felt pen to mark six dots on pipe. Dots should be about ½ inch (1.25 cm) apart (sketch b).

▲ Have a friend hold flute while you hammer a nail into each marked spot. Pound carefully, just enough to make a small hole (sketch b).

▲ Cover all six holes with fingers as you hold flute (sketch c).

▲ Blow into flute in such a way that your breath is split by the notch. It will sound like a whistle. (This may take some practice.)

▲ Play different notes by blowing into flute and lifting fingers off holes.

Life in Bible Times: In Bible Times, every shepherd owned a simple pipe or flute made from two hollowed-out pieces of cane. They would play their flutes to help pass the time while out watching their goats or sheep. Also, flutes were played along with other instruments as a way of worshiping God.

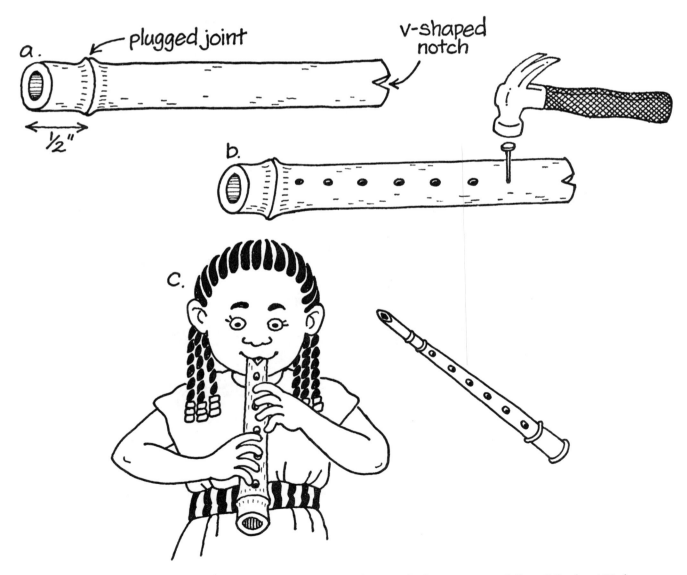

"Praise him with tambourine and dancing, praise him with the strings and flute." Psalm 150:4

PIPES
(30 MINUTES)

Materials: Bamboo (see p. 7 for ordering information), saw, measuring stick, jute or twine, scissors, masking tape, sandpaper. Optional: If bamboo is not available, use discarded garden hose. If necessary, sterilize hose. Glue cardboard circles on ends to plug them.

Preparation: Use saw to cut five bamboo lengths (each with a plugged joint at one end and open at opposite end), the shortest being 4½ inches (11.25 cm) long and each consecutive length being ½ inch (1.25 cm) longer—one set for each child. Cut jute or twine into 1½-yard (135-cm) lengths—two for each child.

Instruct each child in the following procedures:
▲ Use sandpaper to sand rough edges of bamboo lengths.
▲ Tear off a 12-inch (30-cm) length of tape and lay it on table, sticky side up.
▲ Center bamboo lengths on tape, side by side, from shortest to longest, with open ends of bamboo aligned (sketch a).
▲ Wrap ends of tape around bamboo. (The tape will hold bamboo in place while you are lacing it together.)

▲ Beginning at shortest pipe, center one length of jute around end of bamboo and tie about 1-inch (2.5-cm) from top (sketch b).
▲ Wrap jute around each consecutive pipe, tying to secure (sketch c).
▲ When you reach the last bamboo length, tie jute around pipes a second time, working in the opposite direction (sketch d).
▲ Tie a square knot at the end and cut off excess jute.
▲ Repeat process to secure opposite ends of bamboo.
▲ Remove tape.
▲ To play, blow into bamboo lengths as you would blow into a soda bottle.

Life in Bible Times: **Simple flutes, made from hollowed out pieces of cane, were commonly used in Bible Times. Sometimes several cane pieces were laced together to make an instrument called "pipes." When blown into, each pipe made a different sound according to its length.**

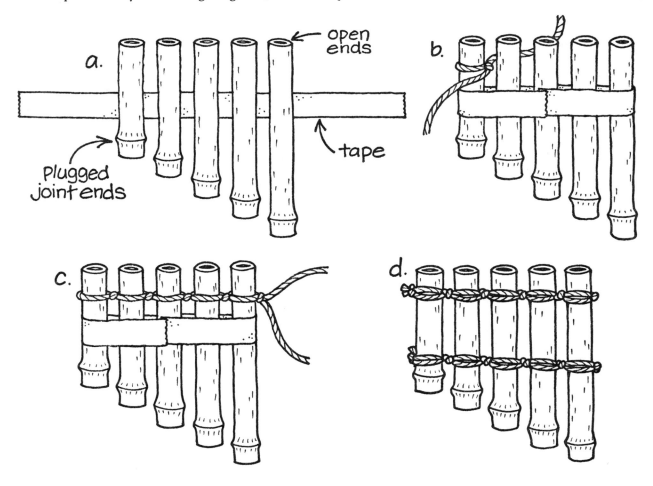

"Praise him with tambourine and dancing, praise him with the strings and flute." Psalm 150:4

FINGER CYMBALS
(5 MINUTES)

Materials: For each child—two large buttons with large holes, two size 14 rubber bands (available at office supply stores), one toothpick.

Instruct each child in the following procedures:

▲ Thread a rubber band through two holes in button (sketch a). If necessary, use toothpick to push rubber band through holes.

▲ Repeat to make second cymbal.

▲ To play, fasten cymbals to your fingers and tap out a rhythm (sketch b).

Life in Bible Times: **In Bible Times, cymbals were a popular instrument used to worship God. They were made of metal and were about the size of dinner plates. When two cymbals were hit together they made a loud crashing sound.**

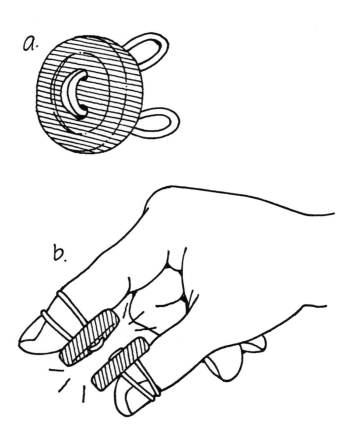

"Praise him with the clash of cymbals, praise him with resounding cymbals." Psalm 150:5

EASY TAMBOURINE
(15 MINUTES)

Materials: Crepe paper streamers, scissors, ruler, hole punches, chenille wires, transparent tape. For each child—one sturdy paper plate and four jingle bells.

Preparation: Cut chenille wires into 4-inch (10-cm) lengths—four for each child. Cut crepe paper into 12-inch (30-cm) lengths—two for each child.

Instruct each child in the following procedures:

▲ Use hole punch to punch four holes around edge of paper plate (see sketch).

▲ Thread a chenille wire piece through one of the holes.

▲ Thread a bell onto chenille wire.

▲ Twist ends of wire together to secure.

▲ Repeat previous three steps to add three more bells to tambourine.

▲ Tape streamers to edge of tambourine.

▲ Tap finger in center or shake tambourine to play.

Life in Bible Times: **In Bible Times, tambourines were played when people got together to celebrate or worship. In a book of the Bible called Psalms, the writer tells people to get out their musical instruments and worship God with music and dancing! What song will you sing to God as you play your tambourine?**

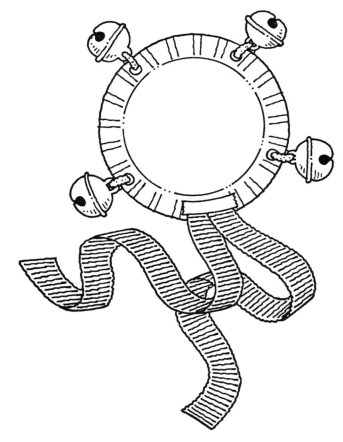

"Let them praise his name with dancing and make music to him with tambourine and harp." Psalm 14:3

BIBLE TIMES WRITING

ANCIENT SCROLL
(30 MINUTES)

Materials: Greek and Hebrew alphabets and/or "Be a Bible Times Scribe" (pp. 39-41), black tempera paint, paintbrushes, shallow plastic containers, yarn or jute, newspapers, scissors, ruler, photocopier. For each child—one brown paper grocery bag.

Preparation: Cut yarn or jute into 1-foot (30-cm) lengths—one for each child. Photocopy Greek and Hebrew alphabets and/or "Be a Bible Times Scribe" pages—one for each child. Pour paint into containers. Cover work area with newspapers.

Instruct each child in the following procedures:

▲ Cut bag to make a rectangular sheet of paper (sketch a).

▲ Crumple sheet (sketch b) and smooth out. Repeat crumpling process several times. (This will give the sheet an ancient look.)

▲ Use paint to copy Hebrew or Greek letters onto crumpled sheet.

▲ Allow to dry.

▲ Roll up sheet and tie with yarn or jute.

Simplification Ideas: Younger elementary children use felt pens to copy a short Bible verse or the word "Shalom" on scrolls. Teacher cuts rectangle for preschoolers. Preschool children use felt pens to draw a picture on scrolls.

Life in Bible Times: **What is our paper made from?** (Trees.) In Bible Times, paper was made from the stems of a plant called papyrus. Papyrus strips were beaten together into long sheets and rolled to make scrolls. Other scrolls were made from parchment—goat or sheep skins that had been dried and stretched.

"[Jesus] went to Nazareth, where he had been brought up, and on the Sabbath day he went into the synagogue, as was his custom. And he stood up to read. The scroll of the prophet Isaiah was handed to him." Luke 4:16,17

TINY CLAY POT AND SCROLL
(30 MINUTES)

Materials: Air-drying clay or self-hardening clay (see p. 51 for recipe), shallow containers of water, pencils, brown paper bags, scissors.

Preparation: Divide clay into 2½-inch (6.25-cm) balls—one for each child.

Instruct each child in the following procedures:

▲ Knead clay to soften, then form a ball.

▲ Press your thumb into clay ball (sketch a).

▲ Leaving thumb in clay, use other fingers to pull clay up to form a small pot (sketch b).

▲ Dip fingertips in water and smooth out any cracks in the surface of the pot.

▲ Use pencil to scratch your initials on bottom of pot.

▲ Allow to dry.

▲ Use scissors to cut a small rectangle from paper bag.

▲ Crumple rectangle and smooth out. Repeat several times to give paper an ancient look (sketch c).

▲ Roll up rectangle like a scroll.

▲ Place scroll inside jar (sketch d).

Enrichment Idea: Older children copy Hebrew or Greek letters onto scroll (see pp. 39-41).

Life in Bible Times: **Not long after Jesus lived on earth, a group of people who lived near the Dead Sea placed Bible scrolls in special jars. The people hid the jars inside nearby caves. After the scrolls were hidden, enemy soldiers chased the people out of their village and destroyed everything they owned. But the hidden scrolls remained safe! In fact, the scrolls remained hidden for almost 2,000 years. Then the scrolls were found by a shepherd who went into a cave looking for his goat. The scrolls are the oldest copies of the Bible ever discovered! The words on the Dead Sea Scrolls translate into the same words we read in our Bibles today. God protected His Word for 2,000 years.**

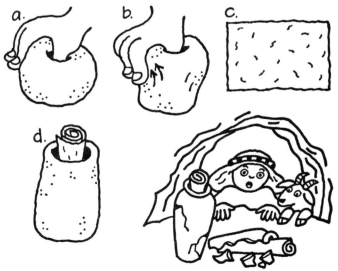

"Your word, O Lord, is eternal; it stands firm in the heavens." Psalm 119:89

THE GREEK ALPHABET

GREEK		ROMAN	GREEK		ROMAN
alpha	A	A	kappa	K	K
bēta	B	B	lambda	L	L
gamma	Γ	G	mu	M	M
delta	△	D	nu	N	N
epsilon	E	E	xi	Ξ	
(digamma) upsilon	Y	FY	omicron	O	O
zēta	Z	Z	pi	Γ	P
ēta	H	H	rhō	P	R
thēta	⊙		sigma	Σ	S
iota	I	I	tau	T	T

The Hebrew Alphabet

(with phonetic values)

Note: The Hebrew alphabet reads from right to left. Also, several Hebrew characters are not included here because they have no English equivalents.

d	g	b	a
ד	ג	ב	א
dalet (DOLL-ed)	gimmal (GEE-mel)	bet (bait)	alef (AH-lif)
h	z	v, w, ō, u	ă, h
ח	ז	ו	ה
chet (khet)	zayin (ZI-on)	vav (vov)	heh (hay)
m	l	k	ē, ĭ, y
מ	ל	כ	י
mem (mem)	lamed (LA-med)	kaf (khaf)	yod (yode)
q	p, f	s	n
ק	פ	ס	ן
qof (qofe)	pe (pay)	samekh (SAM-ekh)	nun (noon)
t	sh	r	
ת	ש	ר	
tav (tav)	shin (sheen)	resh (resh)	

BE A BIBLE TIMES SCRIBE!

Copy Hebrew words onto a scroll or tablet.
(Hebrew is written from right to left!)

Shalom (peace)

שלום

Psalm 33:11
"The plans of the Lord stand firm forever."

עצת יהוה לעולם תעמד

Psalm 100:3
"It is he who made us,

הוא עשנו

and we are his."

ולו אנחנו

The words of the Bible were copied onto scrolls letter by letter.
Imagine how long it took to make a copy of all 66 books of the Bible!

WAXED BOARD AND WRITING STICK
(15 MINUTES)

Materials: Paraffin, corrugated cardboard, scissors, utility knife, ruler, paintbrushes, heating unit (stove, hot plate or camp stove), hot pad, large saucepan, water, cooking oil, paper towels, coffee can and Crockpot. For each child—one craft stick.

Preparation: Cut cardboard into 9-inch (22.5-cm) squares—one for each child. Use utility knife to sharpen one end of each craft stick. Rub oil on inside of coffee can. Use knife to break up paraffin into chunks. Place chunks in oiled can. Heat water to boiling in saucepan. Place can of wax in saucepan and melt paraffin. Pour boiling water into Crockpot and place can of wax into Crockpot. Set Crockpot on medium setting. (Wax is now ready to be used by children.)

Instruct each child in the following procedures:
▲ Use paintbrush to paint cardboard with a thick layer of wax (sketch a). Let dry.
▲ Add a second coat of wax. Let dry.
▲ Use sharpened craft stick to write on waxed board (sketch b).

Enrichment Idea: Older children practice writing Greek and Hebrew letters (see pp. 39-41).

Life in Bible Times: What materials do you use for writing or drawing? In Bible Times, permanent documents like books were written on papyrus or parchment. People wrote notes and practiced writing on pieces of broken pottery or wax-covered boards called tablets. A sharpened reed or stick was used to scratch letters in the tablets. Zechariah may have written on a waxed tablet to announce the name of his son, John the Baptist.

a. b.

wax card-board craft stick

"[Zechariah] asked for a writing tablet, and to everyone's astonishment he wrote, 'His name is John.'" Luke 1:63

CLAY TABLET WITH WRITING STICK
(TWO-DAY PROJECT/15 MINUTES)

Materials: Air-drying clay, rolling pin, pencils, utility knife, table knives. For each child—one craft stick.

Preparations: Divide clay into fist-sized balls. Use utility knife to sharpen one end of each craft stick.

Instruct each child in the following procedures:
DAY ONE:
▲ Flatten ball of clay with your hand.
▲ Use rolling pin to flatten clay into a slab about ½-inch (1.25-cm) thick.
▲ Use table knife to cut slab into a square or rectangular shape.
▲ Use sharpened craft stick to scratch initials onto bottom of tablet.
▲ Allow to dry.
DAY TWO:
▲ After tablet is dry, use sharpened craft stick to scratch letters onto tablet.

Life in Bible Times: If you want to leave a message for someone, what do you do? In Bible Times, people wrote messages, bills and receipts on broken pieces of pottery. God told Isaiah to write an important message on a tablet. Isaiah may have written God's message on clay tablets made from broken pottery.

Hannah, meet me at the well.

sharpened craft stick

"Go now, write [my message] on a tablet for them, inscribe it on a scroll, that for the days to come it may be an everlasting witness." Isaiah 30:8

STONE CARVING
(30 MINUTES)

Materials: Water color dyes (such as Dr. Martin's) and paintbrushes or permanent felt pens in muted colors, utility knife, plastic containers, water, newspapers. For each child—craft stick and a soft rock that can be carved with a stick. Optional: If soft rocks are not available in your area, you can make imitation rocks. You will need a bowl or bucket, a stick for mixing, milk cartons or small frozen food containers to use as molds, plaster of paris, vermiculite (available at garden supply stores), measuring cup and water.

Preparation: Use utility knife to sharpen one end of each craft stick. Cover work area with newspaper. Fill containers with water. Optional: To make imitation rocks, combine the following in a large bowl: 1 cup plaster of paris, ¾ cup vermiculite and ¾ cup water. Mix well and pour into molds. Allow mixture to harden. Peel away molds.

Instruct each child in the following procedures:
▲ Use craft stick to scratch a simple design in the rock.
▲ Paint or color parts of your design. Allow to dry.

Life in Bible Times: **If you were going to draw pictures to put into a time capsule to show what life is like in the 1990s, what would you draw? We can find out about life in Bible Times by looking at pictures carved in stone during that time. Stone carvings often showed scenes from everyday life, such as a woman spinning thread, a family eating or an army going off to battle. What picture of life in Bible Times will you carve into your rock? In the Bible, God is called a rock. In what way is God like a rock?**

"The Lord lives! Praise be to my Rock! Exalted be God my Savior!" Psalm 18:46

PHYLACTERY
(TWO-DAY PROJECT/45 MINUTES)

Materials: Bibles, light brown seam binding, brown paper bags or brown craft paper, scissors, ruler, white glue diluted with water, shallow plastic containers, white paper, fine-tipped felt pens, embroidery thread or yarn. For each child—small cardboard gift box (used for jewelry).

Preparation: Cut seam binding into 30-inch (75-cm) lengths—one for each child. Cut white paper into 2x3-inch (5x7.5-cm) pieces—two for each child. Cut thread or yarn into 8-inch (20-cm) lengths—two for each child. Pour diluted glue into containers.

Instruct each child in the following procedures:
DAY ONE:
▲ Tear brown paper into small pieces about 1x2-inches (2.5x5-cm).
▲ Soak paper pieces in diluted glue.
▲ Smooth soaked paper pieces onto outside of box and lid to cover completely (sketch a). Let dry.
DAY TWO:
▲ Center length of seam binding on bottom of box and glue (sketch b). Let dry.
▲ Look up one or two Scripture verses in the Bible and copy them onto small pieces of paper. (Teacher may want to suggest a particular verse.)
▲ Roll up paper and tie with thread or yarn (sketch c). Place inside box.
▲ Tie phylactery to your forehead.

Life in Bible Times: **A phylactery is a little leather box containing God's commandments written on rolls of parchment. In Bible Times, Jewish men wore phylacteries on their arms and foreheads to remind them of God's words. What helps you remember God's words?**

"Fix these words of mine in your hearts and minds; tie them as symbols on your hands and bind them on your foreheads." Deuteronomy 11:18

SCRIBE'S INKHORN
(TWO-DAY PROJECT/45 MINUTES)

Materials: Brown paper bags or brown craft paper, scissors, glue, masking tape, white glue diluted with water, plastic containers, cardboard, ruler, string, awl, newspaper. For each child—one paper towel tube.

Preparation: Cut cardboard into 2-inch (5-cm) circles—one for each child. Cut string into 6-inch (15-cm) lengths—one for each child. Cut additional string into 4-inch (10-cm) lengths—one for each child. Cut tubes into 6-inch (15-cm) lengths—one for each child. Pour diluted glue into plastic containers. Cover work area with newspaper.

Instruct each child in the following procedures:

DAY ONE:

▲ Cut several 2-inch (5-cm) slashes halfway around bottom of tube (sketch a).

▲ Press slashed side toward unslashed slide and tape to form diagonal point at end of tube (sketch b).

▲ Wrinkle brown paper to soften. Tear into strips about 1 inch (2.5 cm) wide.

▲ Soak strips in diluted white glue. Apply strips to tube to cover completely (sketch c).

▲ Glue shorter length of string around the edge of the cardboard circle (sketch d).

▲ Cover both sides of cardboard circle (and string) with brown paper strips.

▲ Let dry.

DAY TWO:

▲ Use awl to poke two holes in lid and two holes in center back of inkhorn (sketch e).

▲ Thread longer length of string through all four holes and tie to attach lid to horn (sketch f). The rim (string) side of cap should facedown.

▲ Tuck inkhorn in your belt.

Life in Bible Times: In Bible Times, many people didn't know how to read or write. If a person needed to write a letter, he would go to the local scribe, who sat in the marketplace or some other public place. Sometimes a scribe carried a horn filled with ink on his belt. The ink was made of carbon from charcoal, mixed with oil and water. A scribe's "pen" was made from a piece of reed or rush. Besides writing letters, scribes were also hired to copy the Scriptures. It took a long time to make an entire copy of the Bible. That's why every copy was very precious.

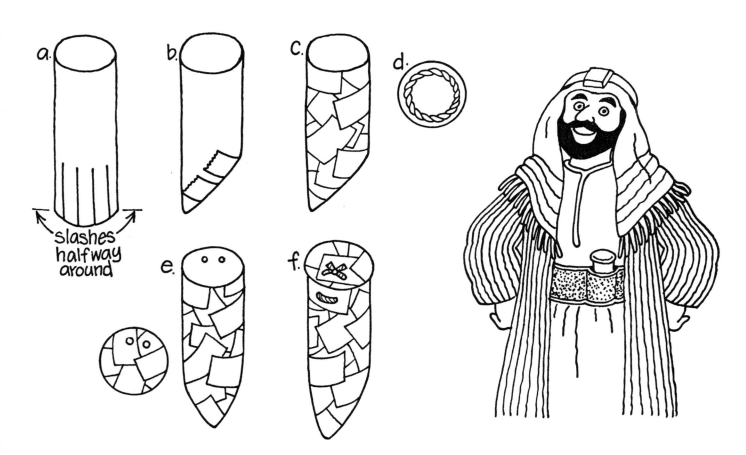

"Baruch replied, '[Jeremiah] dictated all these words to me, and I wrote them in ink on the scroll.'" Jeremiah 36:18

BIBLE TIMES BASKETS, MATS AND POTS

WOVEN PAPER MAT
(30 MINUTES)

Materials: Brightly colored construction paper in 9x12-inch (22.5x30-cm) sheets, scissors, glue, pencil, ruler.

Preparation: Fold sheet of construction paper in half width-wise—one for each child. Measure and draw slit lines along folded edge at 1-inch (2.5-cm) intervals, stopping 1 inch (2.5 cm) from edge of paper (sketch a). Cut contrasting colored construction paper into 1½x9-inch (3.75 22.5-cm) strips—six for each child.

Instruct each child in the following procedures:

▲ Cut along slit lines on folded sheet of construction paper.

▲ Unfold paper.

▲ With teacher's help, weave a strip of paper through slits—over and under, over and under, etc. (sketch b).

▲ Weave a second strip through slits—under and over, under and over, etc.

▲ Weave remaining strips through slits, alternating pattern with each strip (sketch c).

▲ Glue ends of strips to edges of paper.

Life in Bible Times: **What are your clothes made of? In Bible Times, clothes were made from sheep's wool. Weavers used wooden looms to weave the wool thread into cloth. How long did it take you to weave your mat? How long do you think it would take to weave small threads into a piece of cloth big enough for a tunic?**

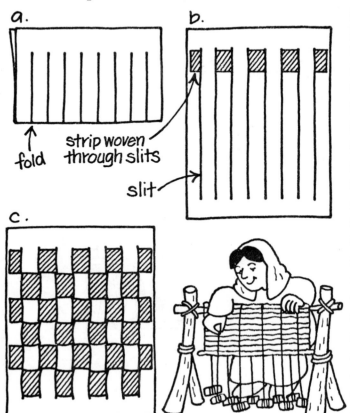

"For Aaron and his sons, they made tunics of fine linen—the work of a weaver." Exodus 39:27

SIMPLE WOVEN BASKET
(30 MINUTES)

Materials: Brightly colored yarn, scissors, measuring stick. For each child—one plastic berry basket.

Preparation: Cut yarn into 1-yard (90-cm) lengths—several for each child.

Instruct each child in the following procedures:

▲ With teacher's help, tie a length of yarn to top corner of basket (sketch a).

▲ Weave yarn in and out of holes around basket (sketch b). It isn't necessary to tie end of yarn to basket.

▲ Repeat first two steps to weave additional yarn lengths around basket (sketch c).

Life in Bible Times: **Where do you keep your toys? Your clothes? In Bible Times, children kept their toys in baskets made of reeds and grasses. Food was stored in baskets, too. One time Paul was hiding from some men who wanted to hurt him. His friends lowered him out of a window in a big basket!**

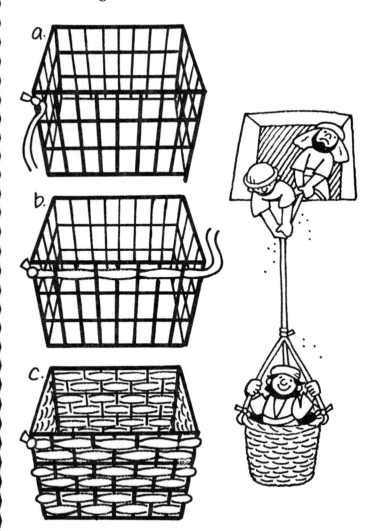

"His followers took him by night and lowered him in a basket through an opening in the wall." Acts 9:25

WOVEN CLOTH MAT
(30 MINUTES)

Materials: Burlap, yarn in a variety of colors, scissors, measuring stick, drill, 3/16-inch (.45-cm) drill bit. For each child—one craft stick.

Preparation: Cut burlap into 11x17-inch (27.5x42.5-cm) rectangles—one for each child. Cut yarn into 15-inch (37.5-cm) lengths—about ten for each child. Drill a hole in the end of each craft stick.

Instruct each child in the following procedures:

▲ Thread one length of yarn onto craft stick (sketch a).

▲ Pull out four consecutive threads from anywhere on long edge of burlap to create an open space (sketch b).

▲ Leading with craft stick, weave in and out of threads in this open space (sketch c).

▲ Repeat previous three steps to weave additional strands of yarn into burlap (sketch d).

Simplification Idea: For younger children, teacher pulls threads from burlap ahead of time.

Life in Bible Times: **In Bible Times, most cloth was made from sheep's wool. The wool was cut from the sheep, combed, washed and dyed. Next, the wool was spun on a spindle, twisting the wool fibers into yarn. Then the yarn was woven into cloth on a wooden loom. Many times clothing, blankets and mats were made from a single, uncut piece of cloth.**

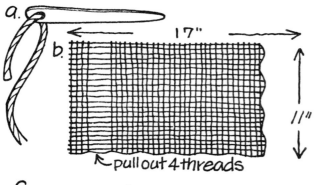

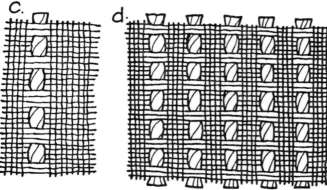

"When the soldiers crucified Jesus, they took his clothes, dividing them into four shares, one for each of them, with the undergarment remaining. This garment was seamless, woven in one piece from top to bottom." John 19:23

REED MAT
(30 MINUTES)

Materials: Scissors, 5/8-inch (1.5-cm) flat reed (see p. 7 for ordering information), measuring stick, glue, bucket of water, towel.

Preparation: Cut reed into 11-inch (27.5-cm) lengths—eight for each child. Cut additional reed into 14-inch (35-cm) lengths—14 for each child. Soak reed lengths in bucket of water for 3-5 minutes.

Instruct each child in the following procedures:

▲ Place the eight shorter reed lengths in front of you with "fuzzy" side down (sketch a). Leave a 1/2-inch (1.25-cm) space between each reed.

▲ Weave a longer reed length over and under, over and under the eight lengths (sketch a).

▲ Next to first woven reed length, weave a second reed length under and over, under and over the eight lengths.

▲ Repeat process to add remaining reed lengths, alternating weaving pattern with each reed you add (sketch b).

▲ Glue outside edges of mat together to secure. Let dry.

Life in Bible Times: **Where do you like to lie down to rest? In Bible Times, people often rested on woven mats made from grasses or reeds. After Jesus healed a lame man, He told the man to get up, take his mat and go home.**

"He got up, took his mat and walked out in full view of them all. This amazed everyone and they praised God, saying, 'We have never seen anything like this!'" Mark 2:12

REED BASKET
(60 MINUTES)

Materials: Bucket of water, ⅜-inch (.9-cm) flat reed, (see p. 7 for ordering information), ¼-inch (.6-cm) flat oval reed, ¼-inch (.6-cm) flat reed, scissors, measuring stick, towel, clothespins.

Preparation: Cut ⅜-inch (.9-cm) flat reed into 12-inch (30-cm) lengths—eight for each child. These will be the spokes. Cut additional ⅜-inch (.9-cm) flat reed into 18-inch (45-cm) lengths—two for each child. Cut ¼-inch (.6-cm) flat oval reed into 6-foot (1.8-m) lengths—two for each child. Cut ¼-inch (.6-cm) flat reed into 36-inch (90-cm) lengths—one for each child. Soak all reeds in bucket of water for 3-5 minutes. Note: If reeds become dry as children are working, dip in water to keep pliable.

Instruct each child in the following procedures:

▲ Bend a length of reed and feel its texture. The fuzzy side is the "wrong" side. As you work, keep the wrong side inside basket.

▲ Lay four spokes vertically in front of you with the fuzzy side up, about ¼-inch (1.25-cm) apart (sketch a).

▲ Add remaining four spokes by weaving horizontally through center of first spokes (sketch b).

▲ Woven area should be a 3-inch (7.5-cm) square. This is the base of the basket. Bend up spokes perpendicular to the base (sketch c).

▲ Beginning close to base of basket, weave oval reed in and out all the way around once (sketch d).

▲ When you reach the spoke where you started, split the spoke in half and continue weaving oval reed around basket (sketch e).

▲ To add second oval reed, overlap previous reed by three or four spokes and continue weaving around basket.

▲ Continue weaving until basket is about 2½-inches (6.25-cm) tall. Stop weaving at same spoke with which you began.

▲ Use scissors to trim spokes which are inside basket even with top of basket (sketch f).

▲ Trim spokes which are outside basket to a point and bend to inside of basket, inserting behind oval reed (sketch f).

▲ Wrap 18-inch (45-cm) reed lengths around inside and outside of basket edge to form rim. Hold in place with clothespins (sketch g).

▲ Insert end of 36-inch (90-cm) flat reed inside rim and lace around rim to attach rim to basket (sketch h).

▲ After lacing around entire rim of basket, tuck end of lacing under rim and under a spoke.

Life in Bible Times: **In Bible Times, baskets were a common sight. They were made from grasses and reeds that grew along riverbanks. What Bible story can you think of that mentions baskets? Once, after Jesus miraculously fed a large crowd of people, the leftover bread and fish were gathered into baskets.**

"So they gathered them and filled twelve baskets with the pieces of the five barley loaves left over by those who had eaten." John 6:13

BRAIDED MAT
(60 MINUTES)

Materials: Jute in a variety of colors, heavy duty thread, scissors, measuring stick, T-pins. For each child—one board (wood, foam core, cork, etc.) at least 5-inches (12.5-cm) square, one large needle.

Preparation: Cut jute into 4-yard (3.6-m) lengths—three for each child.

Instruct each child in the following procedures:

▲ Use thread to tie three lengths of jute together at one end (sketch a).

▲ Use T-pins to attach tied end to center of board. Then braid a portion of the three strands of jute (sketch b).

▲ Wind braided jute in a circular or oval shape (sketch c). Use T-pins to secure mat to board.

▲ Braid another section of jute. Wind braided portion and use pins to attach to board.

▲ Repeat previous step until all jute as been used.

▲ Thread needle. Beginning at center of mat, stitch through jute to outer edge of mat (sketch d).

▲ Repeat previous step at least six times, until mat is held together firmly.

▲ Remove T-pins and turn mat over (sketch e).

Life in Bible Times: What is your favorite room in your house or apartment? Where is your favorite place to sit? Bible Times homes usually had only one room. And that one room didn't contain much furniture. Often people sat and slept on mats. These mats were made from strands of straw or grasses that were woven or braided together. Sometimes the straw was dyed so each mat had its own unique colorful pattern.

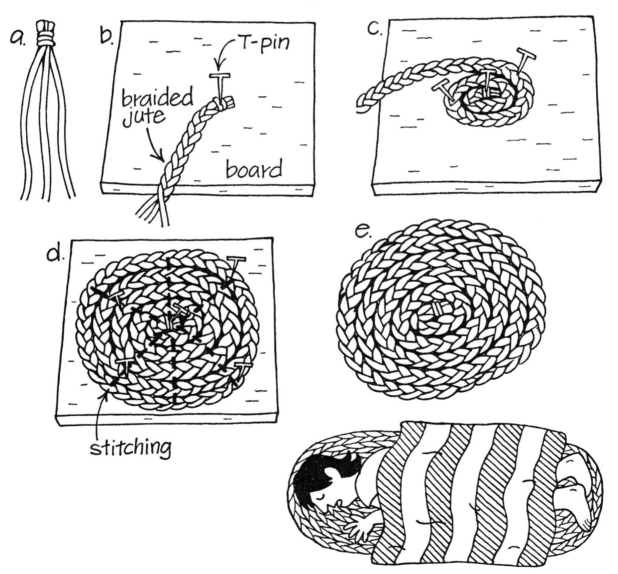

"In the evening Uriah went out to sleep on his mat among his master's servants." 2 Samuel 11:13

OIL LAMP
(15 MINUTES)

Materials: Air-drying or self-hardening clay (see p. 51 for recipe), cotton sheeting, pencils, scissors, ruler, shallow containers of water. Optional—pottery clay, kiln, olive oil, matches. (If lamp is to be used, it must be fired in a kiln.)

Preparation: Divide clay into 3-inch (7.5-cm) balls—one for each child. Cut sheeting into 1x4-inch (2.5x10-cm) strips—one for each child.

Instruct each child in the following procedures:

▲ Press thumb into clay ball (sketch a).
▲ Shape lamp by pulling sides out from center (sketch b).
▲ Pinch one end together to make a handle (sketch c).
▲ Pull out lip of opposite end to make a spout (sketch c).
▲ Wet your fingertips in water and smooth out any cracks in the surface of the lamp.
▲ Use pencil to scratch initials into the bottom of lamp.
▲ Allow to dry. Optional—fire lamp in kiln.
▲ Place cloth strip in lamp for wick.
▲ If lamp has been fired, pour olive oil into lamp. Allow oil to soak through wick. Teacher uses match to light wick.

Life in Bible Times: In Bible Times, there was no electricity. At night, homes were lighted with small clay oil lamps. Fuel for the lamps was made from olives. The wicks were made from cotton or linen cloth.

Jesus is like a light. Without Him we can't "see" or understand the truth. With Jesus' help we can understand truth about God, ourselves and others.

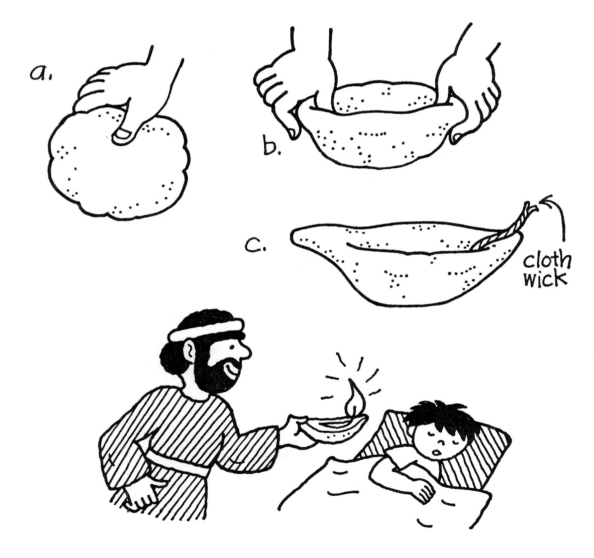

"I have come into the world as a light, so that no one who believes in me should stay in darkness." John 12:46

COIL POT
(30 MINUTES)

Materials: Air-drying or self-hardening clay (see p. 51 for recipe), forks, knives, sponges, shallow containers of water.

Instruct each child in the following procedures:

▲ Knead clay to soften.

▲ Use a portion of clay to make a circular base about ¼-inch (1.25-cm) thick (sketch a).

▲ Roll remaining clay into several ½-inch (1.25-cm) thick coils.

▲ Use fork to score edges of base (sketch b).

▲ Dip sponge in water and rub over the scoring to moisten.

▲ Wrap coil around edge of base (sketch c) and pinch bottom end of coil flat so it attaches to base.

▲ Use fork to score top of coil and moisten with sponge. Then add a second coil.

▲ Repeat above step to add additional coils.

▲ Use moistened sponge to smooth sides and top of the pot (sketch d).

▲ Allow to dry.

Life in Bible Times: **In Bible Times, clay pots were used for cooking and storing food and water. A potter dug clay from the ground and mixed it with water to make it soft. He used his hands to make small pots and a potter's wheel to make bigger pots. After shaping a pot, the potter put it in the sun or in an oven to dry.**

"But who are you, O man, to talk back to God? 'Shall what is formed say to him who formed it, "Why did you make me like this?"' Does not the potter have the right to make out of the same lump of clay some pottery for noble purposes and some for common use?" Romans 9:20,21

RECIPES FOR CLAY

SELF-HARDENING CLAY

Materials: Large pot, wooden spoon, heating element, 1 cup sand, ½ cup cornstarch, 1 tsp. powdered alum, ¾ cup hot water. Optional—food coloring.

Instructions: Mix sand, cornstarch and alum in pot. Add hot water and stir vigorously. Add food coloring if desired. Cook over medium heat until thick, stirring constantly. After cooling, store in an airtight container. Mold as desired, then dry in sun for several days. This clay does not need shellac or varnish to protect it. Makes 2 cups.

SAWDUST CLAY

Materials: Large bowl or bucket, wooden spoon, 2 parts fine sawdust (any kind except redwood) to 1 part flour, water.

Instructions: Mix sawdust and flour in bowl or bucket. Adding a little water at a time, stir until mixture reaches a stiff but pliable consistency. Add more flour and water if clay is too crumbly. Knead clay until it becomes elastic and it is easy to shape. Store in an airtight container. Mold as desired, then dry in sun for several days. This clay becomes very hard when air-dried. After drying, clay can be sanded or decorated with paint.

CORNSTARCH DOUGH

Materials: Pot, wooden spoon, heating element, 2 cups cornstarch, 4 cups baking soda, 2½ cups cold water, paper towels, wax paper.

Instructions: Mix cornstarch and baking soda in pot. Add water. Cook and stir over medium heat for about 5 minutes until mixture thickens and resembles mashed potatoes. Remove from heat. Cover pot with a wet paper towel and allow dough to cool. Working on a surface covered with wax paper, knead cooled dough for about 5 minutes. Store in an airtight container. Mold as desired, then dry in sun for several days. Decorate with paint if desired.

Other Neat Stuff from Bible Times

MONEY POUCH AND COINS
(30 MINUTES)

Materials: For pouch—brown felt or vinyl fabric; measuring stick; black felt pen; scissors; hole punch; ⅛-inch (.3-cm) leather or plastic lacing (lanyard). For coins—spherical, lead fish sinkers in various sizes; hammers; nails; a hard surface (such as asphalt or concrete).

Preparation: Trace 12-inch (30-cm) circles onto felt or vinyl and cut out—one for each child. Cut lacing into 1½-yard (135-cm) lengths—two for each child.

Instruct each child in the following procedures:

TO MAKE POUCH:

▲ Use hole punch to make an even number of holes around the outside of the felt circle about 1 inch (2.5 cm) from edge and 1 inch (2.5-cm) apart (sketch a).

▲ Thread one length of lacing through holes (sketch b).

▲ Starting from opposite side of felt circle, thread second length of lacing through the same holes (sketch c).

▲ Gather all four ends of lacing, making sure they are even, and tie a knot (sketch d).

▲ Hold pouch in one hand and pull on lacing with other hand. Circle will close to form pouch (sketch e).

TO MAKE COINS:

▲ Place a lead sinker on hard surface. Use hammer to flatten sinker. (Caution: Children should wash hands after touching lead.)

▲ Repeat to make additional coins.

▲ Use a nail to scratch symbols on your coins (sketch f).

▲ Place coins in pouch. Hang pouch over shoulder.

Life in Bible Times: What do you use to carry your belongings to and from school? In Bible Times, people often carried their small personal belongings in pouches. The pouches had long straps which were worn over one shoulder and across the body. In a typical traveler's pouch you might have found coins, food and even stones for protection against wild animals.

In Jesus' day, it was common for people to use coins to purchase food, clothing and other items at the marketplace. Roman coins were made of gold or silver and often had the head of the Emperor engraved on them. Jewish coins were made of bronze or copper and pictured plants or symbols.

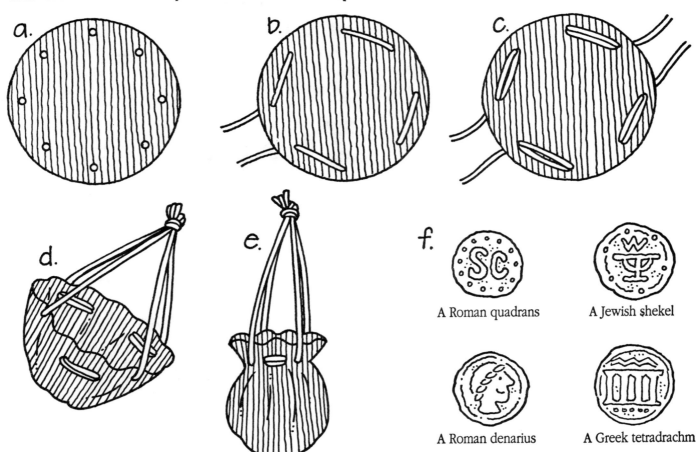

a.

b.

c.

d.

e.

f.

A Roman quadrans

A Jewish shekel

A Roman denarius

A Greek tetradrachm

[Jesus said] "'Show me the coin used for paying the tax.' They brought him a denarius, and he asked them 'Whose portrait is this? And whose inscription?' 'Caesar's,' they replied. Then he said to them, 'Give to Caesar what is Caesar's, and to God what is God's.'" Matthew 22:19-21

MUD BRICKS
(30 MINUTES)

Materials: Saw, ½-inch (1.25-cm) plywood, ruler, hammer, nails, straw, dirt, plastic wading pool, plastic cups, water, wet cloths for clean up.

Preparation: To make brick mold—use saw to cut plywood into 3x5-inch (7.5x12.5-cm) lengths—two for each mold. Cut additional plywood into two 3x10-inch (7.5x25-cm) pieces. Nail plywood pieces together (sketch a). Make one mold for every three or four children.

Instruct each child in the following procedures:

▲ Break a handful of straw into short pieces and place in wading pool.

▲ Add a handful of dirt and about a cup of water. (All children can work together to make a big batch of mud.)

▲ Mix together with feet or hands (sketch b). Add more straw, dirt or water to form a consistency that will stick together.

▲ Pack mud mixture into brick mold (sketch c).

▲ Carefully remove mold from brick.

▲ Allow brick to dry in the sun or in an oven set at a low temperature (sketch d).

Life in Bible Times: What is your house made of? In Bible Times, homes were made from mud bricks. The brickmaker used his feet to mix clay with sand or straw and water. The mixture was then shaped by hand into bricks or pressed into a rectangular wooden mold. The bricks were dried in the sun or baked in a kiln.

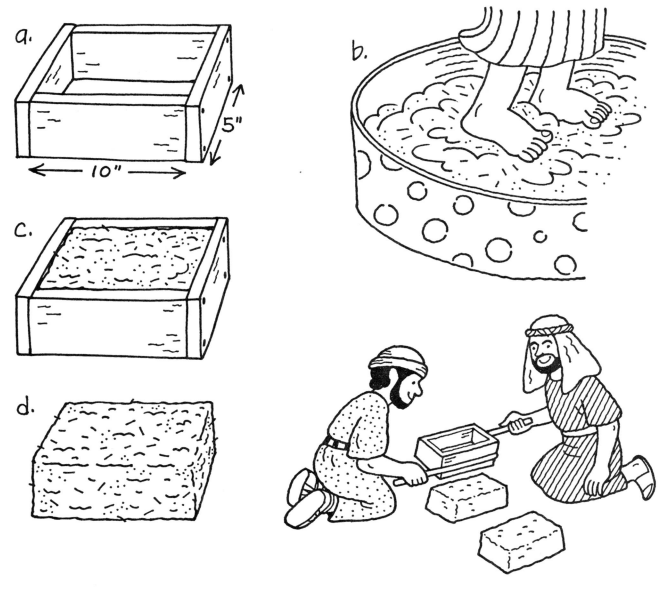

"They said to each other, 'Come, let's make bricks and bake them thoroughly.'" Genesis 11:3

FISHNET
(30 MINUTES)

Materials: Jute or heavy string, scissors, measuring stick.

Preparation: Cut jute into 2-yard (180-cm) lengths—one for each child.

Instruct each child in the following procedures:

▲ Make a loop from jute near one end and tie a square knot (sketch a). This knotted end of jute will be called the "standing end."

▲ Bring "working end" of jute up and through the first loop, forming a second loop below (sketch b). Use left-hand thumb and index finger to pinch working end of jute between strands of original loop.

▲ At point you are pinching with left hand, use right hand to tie a square knot with working end (sketch c).

▲ Pull jute tight to secure (sketch d).

▲ Repeat previous three steps to add the next loop (sketch e).

▲ Continue adding loops until net is desired size (sketch f).

Enrichment Idea: Children use completed nets to play catch with fish shapes cut from large sponges.

Life in Bible Times: Have you ever gone fishing? What equipment did you use to catch fish? Jesus' disciples, Peter, Andrew, James and John, were fishermen on the Sea of Galilee. They used nets to catch fish. The nets had weights tied to them. When the fishermen saw a school of fish in the water, they dropped a net into the water. The weights carried the net down, trapping the fish underneath. Then the fishermen pulled the net full of fish through the water to shore.

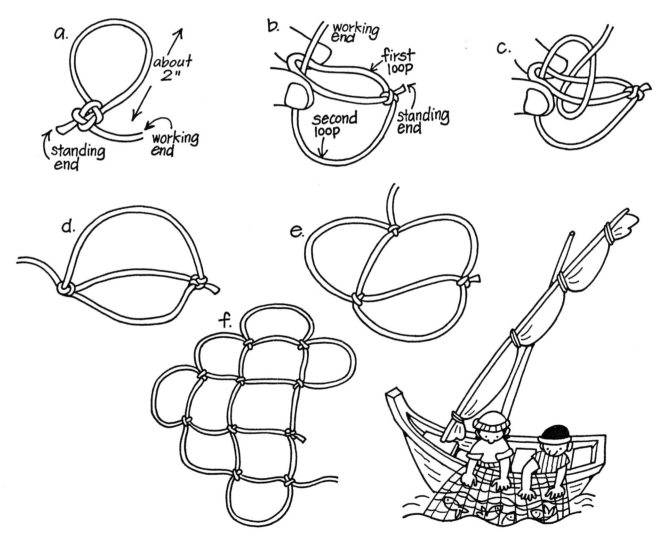

"As Jesus was walking beside the Sea of Galilee, he saw two brothers, Simon called Peter and his brother Andrew. They were casting a net into the lake, for they were fishermen. 'Come, follow me,' Jesus said, 'and I will make you fishers of men.' At once they left their nets and followed him." Matthew 4:18-20

SCALES AND WEIGHTS
(30 MINUTES)

Materials: Lightweight string, ruler, scissors, hole punch, tape, glue. For each child—two tongue depressors, two small plastic cups (like the kind used for condiments), 20 unpopped corn kernels.

Preparation: Cut string into 12-inch (30-cm) lengths—three for each child.

Instruct each child in the following procedures:

▲ Punch two holes opposite each other in each plastic cup (sketch a).

▲ Thread a length of string through the holes in each cup, then knot (sketch b).

▲ Holding center of tongue depressor in one hand, hang one cup on either side. Tape in place (sketch c).

▲ Glue second tongue depressor to first, covering tape.

▲ Tie remaining string tightly around center of two tongue depressors and knot. Knot again at ends to form a loop for holding scale (sketch d).

▲ Hold loop of string in one hand and place corn kernels in cups to balance or unbalance scale.

Life in Bible Times: When you and your family go shopping, how do you pay for your purchases? In the days of the Old Testament, before coins were used, people bought things by trading or by paying a certain weight in gold or silver. Say a person wanted to buy an animal for 50 shekels of silver. A standard weight (a carved stone with its weight inscribed on it) weighing 50 shekels was placed on one side of a scale. Then the buyer placed silver nuggets on the opposite side of the scale until the two sides hung in balance. Some merchants cheated their customers by using standard weights that weighed more or less than they were supposed to. Inspectors visited shopkeepers to make sure their weights were correct.

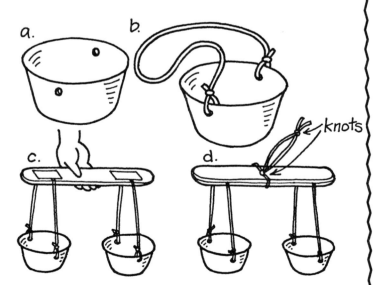

"The Lord abhors dishonest scales, but accurate weights are his delight." Proverbs 11:1.

POTPOURRI IN A POUCH
(30 MINUTES)

Materials: Rose petals; wood shavings; oranges; graters; essence oils such as orange, sandalwood and cinnamon (available at health food and craft supply stores); loosely woven fabric; yarn; ruler; scissors; large plastic needles.

Preparation: Allow rose petals to dry in the sun or in an oven set on "warm" temperature. Cut fabric into 10-inch (25-cm) circles—one for each child. Cut yarn into 2-foot (60-cm) lengths—one for each child.

Instruct each child in the following procedures:

▲ Thread needle with length of yarn.

▲ Sew large running stitches around edge of cloth circle, about 1 inch (2.5 cm) from edge (sketch a).

▲ Pull both ends of yarn to loosely gather circle and form a pouch (sketch b).

▲ Place a handful of rose petals and wood shavings inside pouch.

▲ Grate some orange peel into pouch (as much as you like).

▲ Sprinkle one or two drops of scented oil onto mixture in pouch. Mix petals, shavings and peel with hand to spread scent throughout.

▲ Pull yarn tight to close pouch and tie a bow (sketch c).

Simplification Idea: For preschool children, teacher holds fabric as child sews around edge. Teacher holds grater as child moves orange up and down to grate.

Life in Bible Times: What scents do you like to smell? (Cookies baking, the earth after a rain, flowers, popcorn popping, baby powder.) In Bible Times, an apothecary was a person who made perfumes, cosmetics and medicines. He collected plants, spices and even bark to make sweet smelling mixtures. The mixtures were used for medicine, makeup, perfume, incense and oils.

"Then the Lord said to Moses, 'Take the following fine spices: 500 shekels of liquid myrrh, half as much (that is, 250 shekels) of fragrant cinnamon, 250 shekels of fragrant cane, 500 shekels of cassia—all according to the sanctuary shekel—and a hin of olive oil. Make these into a sacred anointing oil, a fragrant blend, the work of a perfumer.'" Exodus 30:22-25

TORCH
(30 MINUTES)

Materials: Bamboo (see p. 7 for ordering information) or 1-inch (2.5-cm) doweling, saw, pencils, measuring sticks, scissors, brown paper bags, large plastic or paper cups, transparent tape, glue, hot glue gun, glue sticks, cardboard, red, yellow and orange crepe paper streamers.

Preparation: Saw bamboo or doweling into 1-yard (90-cm) lengths—one for each child. Trace around bottom of cup onto cardboard and cut out circle—one for each child. Glue a cardboard circle to one end of each bamboo or dowel length (sketch a). Let it dry. Cut the streamers into 2-yard (180-cm) lengths—one of each color for each child. From brown paper bags, cut rectangles to be wrapped around plastic cups (see sketch b)—one for each child.

Instruct each child in the following procedures:

▲ Wrap brown paper rectangle around cup and tape to secure (sketch b).

▲ Cut streamers at an angle into various lengths which are slightly taller than the cup (sketch c).

▲ Squeeze a line of glue along bottoms of streamers.

▲ Placing longer streamers in the center and shorter streamers around the edge, glue inside cup for "flames" (sketch d).

▲ Teachers use hot glue gun to glue bottom of cup to cardboard circle on the end of bamboo. Let dry.

Life in Bible Times: **When you go out on a dark night, how do you see where you're going? In Bible Times, a person walking at night sometimes carried a torch. The night Jesus was arrested, He prayed in the Garden of Gethsemane. Judas led soldiers into the garden. The soldiers carried torches as they came to arrest Jesus.**

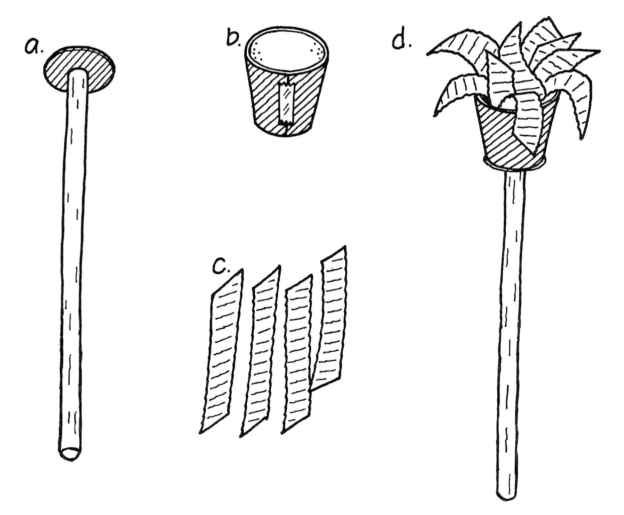

"So Judas came to the grove, guiding a detachment of soldiers and some officials from the chief priests and Pharisees. They were carrying torches, lanterns and weapons." John 18:3

CHAINS
(30 MINUTES)

Materials: Scissors, craft knife, staplers and staples, ruler, silver spray paint, yarn, hole punch. For each child—two paper towel tubes or five toilet paper tubes, newspapers.

Preparation: Use craft knife to cut tubes into 1-inch (2.5-cm) hoops (sketch a). Spray paint hoops.

Instruct each child in the following procedures:

▲ Cut an opening in each hoop (sketch b).

▲ With the exception of two, link hoops together and staple to form a chain (sketch c).

▲ Punch a hole in each end hoop (sketch d).

▲ Punch a hole in each of the two remaining hoops.

▲ Use yarn to link end hoops to chain.

▲ Wear chains by placing an end hoop on each wrist.

Life in Bible Times: After Jesus went to heaven, His disciples traveled to many cities telling people the good news about Jesus. The leaders in some cities didn't want the disciples to talk about Jesus. They ordered the disciples to be put in jail with chains on their hands and feet.

"Peter was sleeping between two soldiers, bound with two chains, and sentries stood guard at the entrance. Suddenly an angel of the Lord appeared and a light shone in the cell. He struck Peter on the side and woke him up. 'Quick, get up!' he said, and the chains fell off Peter's wrists." Acts 12:6,7

KING'S FAN
(30 MINUTES)

Materials: Bamboo (see p. 7 for ordering information) or 1-inch (2.5-cm) doweling, measuring stick, craft glue, transparent tape, scissors, lightweight cardboard, twine, saw. For each child—two sheets of 11x17-inch (27.5x42.5-cm) green construction paper.

Preparation: Saw the bamboo or doweling into 1-yard (90-cm) lengths—one for each child. Cut the twine into 1-yard (90-cm) lengths—one for each child. Cut the cardboard into 1x6-inch (2.5x15-cm) strips—two for each child.

Instruct each child in the following procedures:

▲ Tape two sheets of the construction paper end-to-end (sketch a).
▲ Fold construction paper into 1-inch (2.5-cm) accordion folds (sketch b).
▲ Place glue on half of each cardboard strip and attach a strip to each end of construction paper (sketch c). Let dry.
▲ Lay top 3 inches (7.5 cm) of bamboo on bottom center of fan and glue to secure (sketch d). Let dry.
▲ To secure fan to bamboo, wrap twine around cardboard strips and bamboo (sketch e). Knot ends.
▲ Spread out folds of the fan (sketch f). Wave to create a cool breeze.

Life in Bible Times: What do you like to do to cool off on a hot day? In Bible Times, there was no air conditioning. Fans made from ostrich feathers or palm fronds were used to keep air circulating and create cool breezes. On a warm day, a king might instruct a servant to fan him. If the servant willingly obeyed, he was considered wise.

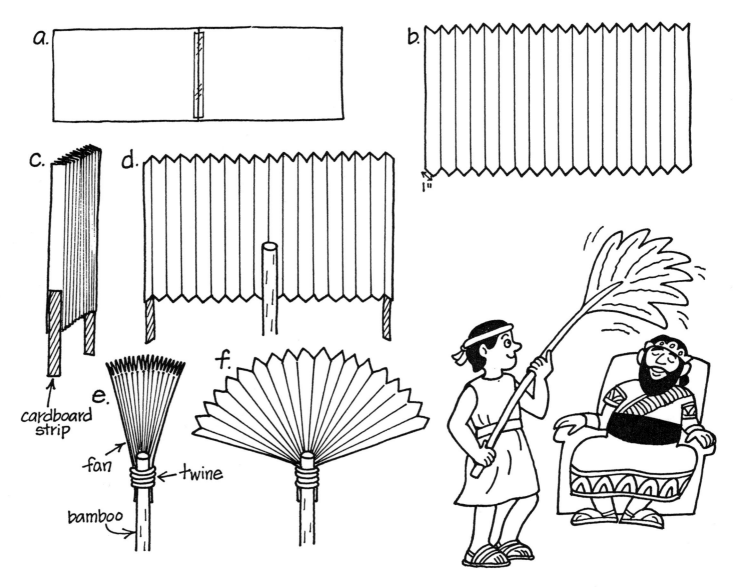

"A king delights in a wise servant." Proverbs 14:35

REPRODUCIBLE
PAGES

BIBLE TIMES GIRL PUPPET (FRONT)

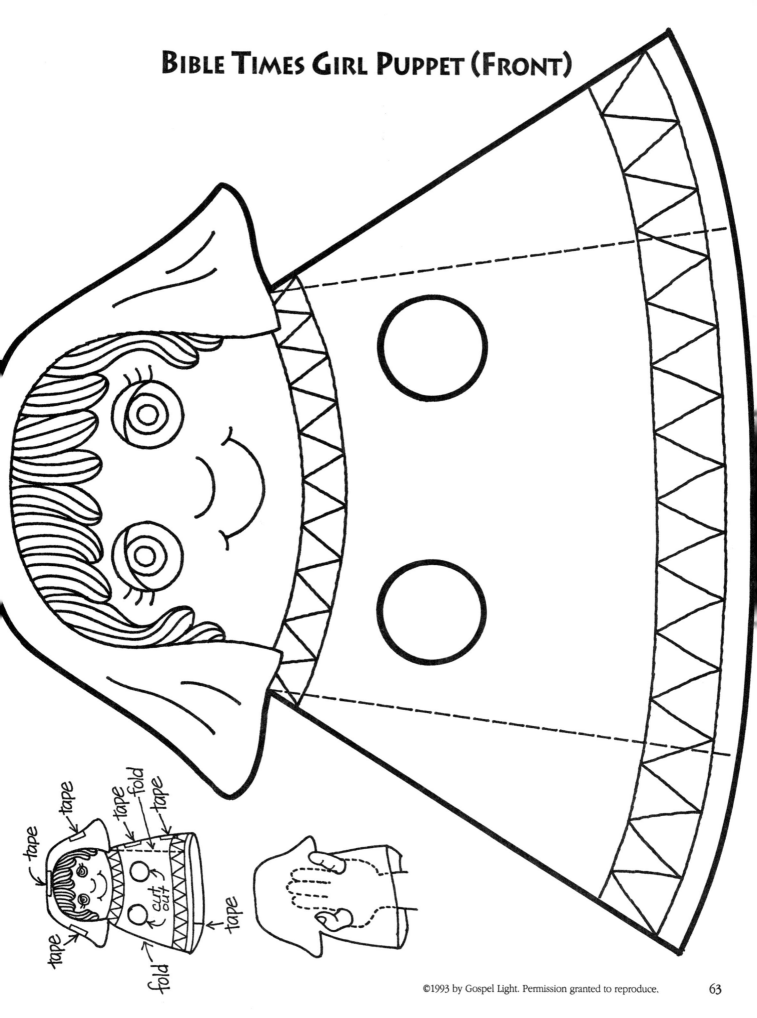

BIBLE TIMES GIRL PUPPET (BACK)

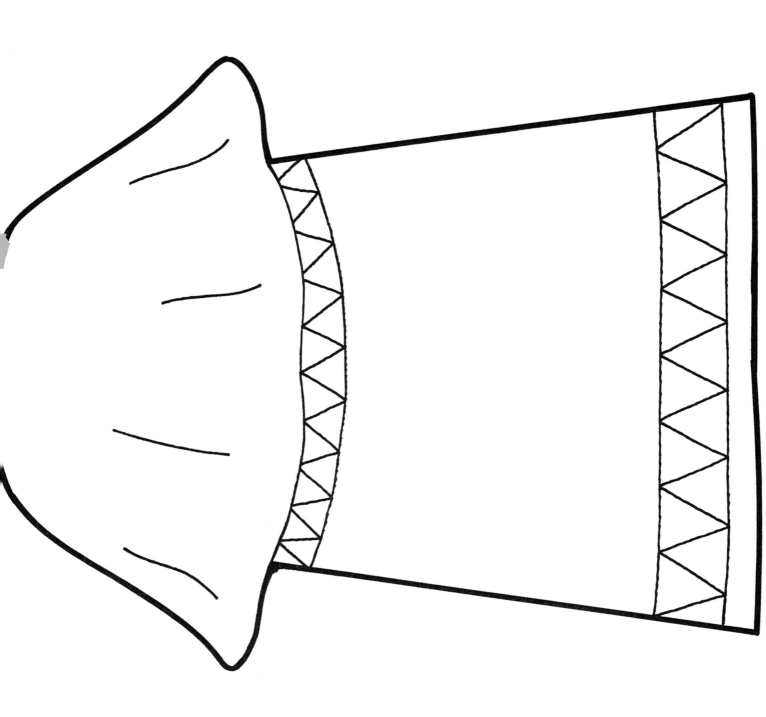

BIBLE TIMES BOY PUPPET (FRONT)

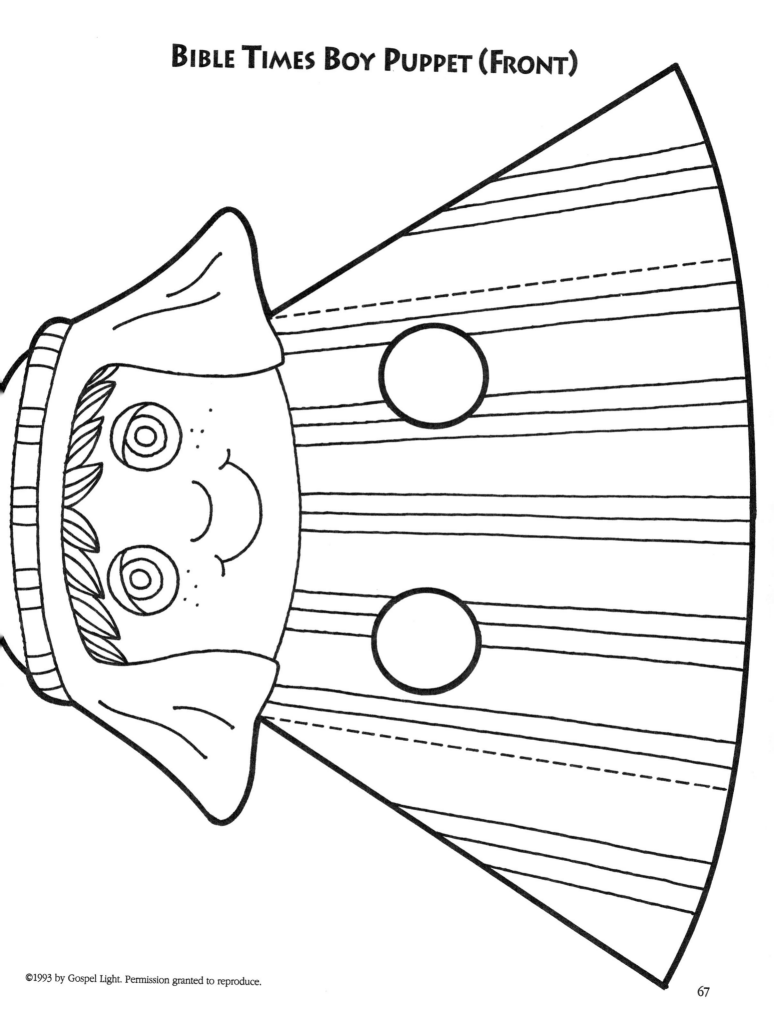

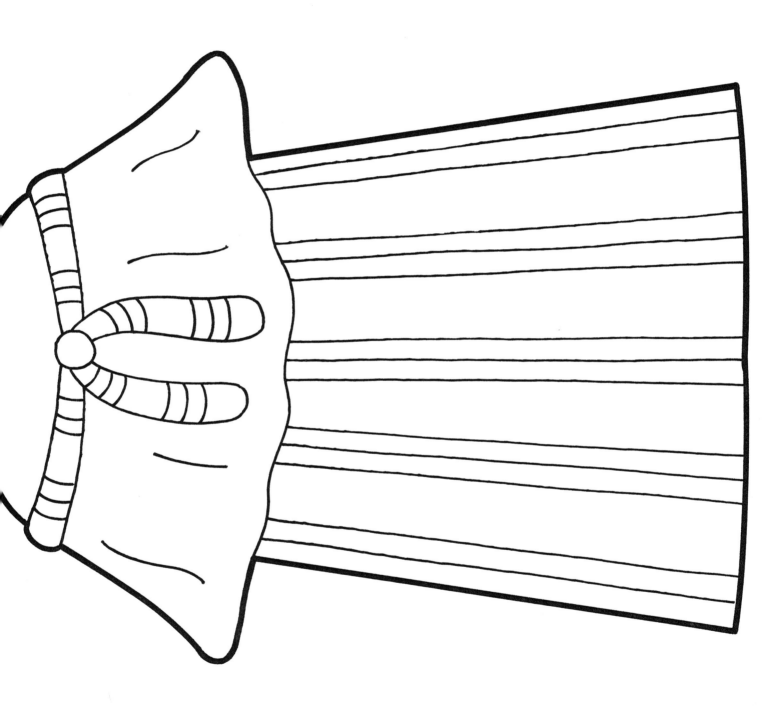

"The plans of the Lord stand firm forever." Psalm 33:11

"Know that the Lord is God. It is he who made us, and we are his." Psalm 100:3

"Blessed is the man who trusts in the Lord." Jeremiah 17:7

"God will be with you wherever you go." Joshua 1:9

"I believe in your commands." Psalm 119:66

Love God. Love your neighbor.

"Praise the Lord. How good it is to sing praises to our God." Psalm 147:1

"For to us a child is born, to us a son is given." Isaiah 9:6

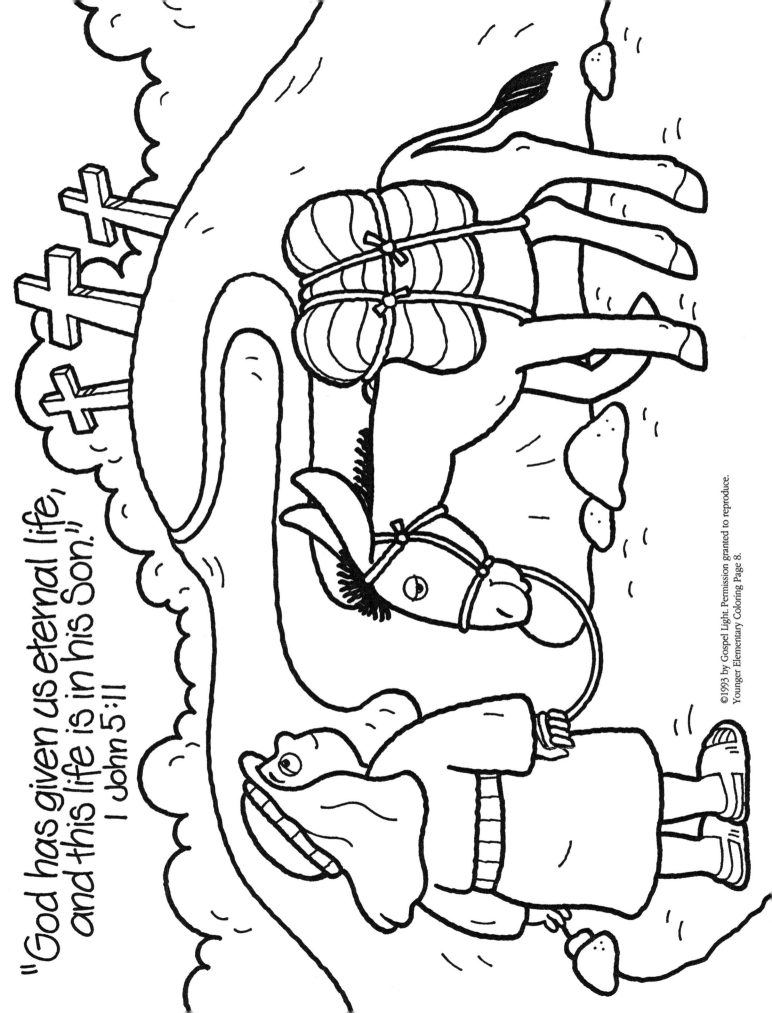

"God has given us eternal life, and this life is in his Son." I John 5:11

"Now you are the body of Christ, and each one of you is a part of it." I Corinthians 12:27

"I am going...to prepare a place for you." John 14:3

"The plans of the Lord stand firm forever, the purposes of his heart through all generations." Psalm 33:11

"Know that the Lord is God. It is he who made us, and we are his." Psalm 100:3

"Blessed is the man who trusts in the LORD, whose confidence is in him." —Jeremiah 17:7

"Be strong and courageous...do not be discouraged, for the Lord your God will be with you wherever you go." Joshua 1:9

"Teach me knowledge and good judgment, for I believe your commands." Psalm 119:66

"Praise the Lord. How good it is to sing praises to our God, how pleasant and fitting to praise him."

Psalm 147:1

"For to us a child is born, to us a son is given...And he will be called Wonderful Counselor, Mighty God, Everlasting Father, Prince of Peace." Isaiah 9:6

"God has given us eternal life, and this life is in his Son." I John 5:11

"Now you are the body of Christ, and each one of you is a part of it."
I Corinthians 12:27

"And if I go and prepare a place for you, I will come back and take you to be with me that you also may be where I am." John 14:3

We're glad God created you!

"It is he who made us and we are his."
Psalm 100:3

SHALOM

we're glad you came to

THIS IS TO CERTIFY THAT

_____

MEMORIZED ALL THE BIBLE MEMORY VERSES AT

_____

_____

thanks for playing your part at

_____

THIS SPECIAL AWARD IS GIVEN TO

_____

FOR

_____

_____

MADE A **UNIQUE** CONTRIBUTION TO OUR GROUP BY

_____

"Now you are the body of Christ,
and each one of you is a part of it."
1 Corinthians 12:27

ATTENDANCE AWARD

presented to

_____

for attendance at

_____

Place sticker here

Place sticker here

Place sticker here

Place sticker here

Place sticker here

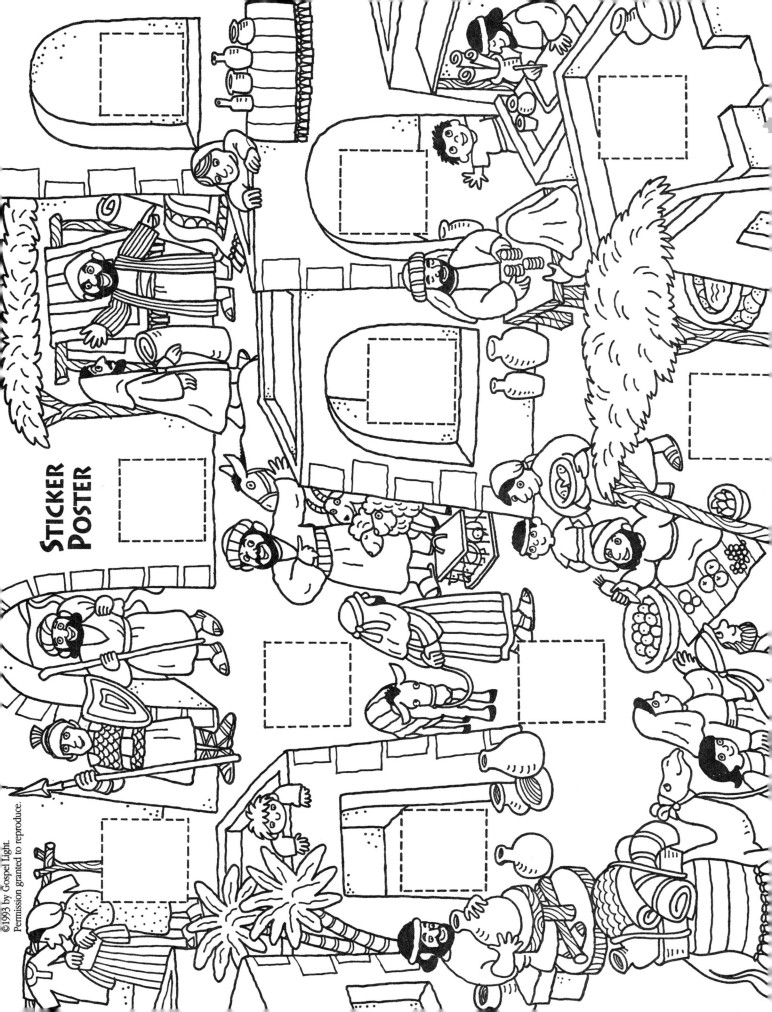

STICKER POSTER